MODERN CHINESE

MODERN CHINESE

70+ easy, everyday recipes from the winner of MasterChef NZ

SAM LOW

ALLEN&UNWIN
SYDNEY·MELBOURNE·AUCKLAND·LONDON

First published in 2023

Text © Sam Low, 2023
Photography © Melanie Jenkins (Flash Studios) and Vanessa Wu
Illustrations © Aan Chu

All rights reserved. No part of this book may be reproduced or transmitted in any form or by any means, electronic or mechanical, including photocopying, recording or by any information storage and retrieval system, without prior permission in writing from the publisher.

Allen & Unwin
Level 2, 10 College Hill, Freemans Bay
Auckland 1011, New Zealand
Phone: (64 9) 377 3800
Email: auckland@allenandunwin.com
Web: www.allenandunwin.co.nz
83 Alexander Street
Crows Nest NSW 2065, Australia
Phone: (61 2) 8425 0100

A catalogue record for this book is available from the National Library of New Zealand.

ISBN 978 1 99100 639 4

Design by Megan van Staden
Food styling by Jo Bridgford and Sam Low
Garments by Steven Junil Park, 6 x 4
Set in Moderat and Galaxie Copernicus

Printed and bound in China by 1010 Printing Ltd

10 9 8 7 6 5 4 3 2 1

I dedicate this book to my parents Hon Chong Low and Fong Siu Fong Low, who never really had the opportunity to properly assimilate into a complex and multicultural country, giving up everything for me and my brothers to pursue opportunities they never had. They continue to teach me the importance of tradition, hardship, resilience, sacrifice and delicious food.

To the queer and the New Zealand Asian community, who showed me that my charisma, uniqueness, nerve and talent are worthy of celebration.

Contents

From the Beginning	9
'Chineseness'	12
Queer Food	14
Kitchen Equipment	19
Cooking Techniques	23
Building Your Chinese Pantry	25
How to Use this Book	32
Apps, Bites & Snacks	35
'Patience' by Chris Tse	67
Soups & Broths	69
Veges, Tofu & Eggs	85
Rice & Noodles	121
'Because There Are Things We Cannot Say' by Nathan Joe	142
Seafood	145
Meat	167
Sauces & Dressings	191
Sweet Things	205
Thank You	233
Index	236

From the Beginning

I was born in Fiji. My parents owned a noodle factory so I was surrounded by the smell of wheat, wontons and noodles; I loved jumping on sacks of flour, getting covered in the stuff. The workers would pack noodles in little tins and we'd bake them in gigantic ovens. One of my earliest food memories was hassling the workers for a taste of the roti and curry they brought from home for their lunches. My parents kept telling me off but I couldn't help myself.

I was eight when we moved to New Zealand and my parents bought a dairy in West Auckland that supplied food to the largely Pasifika community. Customers could buy taro, green bananas, cassava, bok choy and kava. Later, my parents took over a takeaway outlet in the Māngere town centre, Juan's Polynesian Takeaway. They worked all hours selling Polynesian and Chinese fare, including roasted pigs' heads, coconut cream and taro leaf.

I helped out from about age 15, the first time I'd cooked in a commercial environment. I worked the wok station, filling up the bain-maries with green beans and lamb belly stir-fries and Island-style Chinese chop suey. I loved that what I was eating on a daily basis was so varied, so full of life and spices and flavours. I began to understand flavour balance, and I think this was the first time I really made my parents proud. I have never seen food as having a hierarchy. Every cuisine has something to be celebrated.

So, growing up, I was constantly around food and cooking but it was not until high school that it became clear that this was something I had a real affinity for. I attended hospitality classes, worked part time at the Auckland Seafood School down by the waterfront, and completed a food and beverage apprenticeship at SkyCity.

SkyCity was where I discovered coffee. At the time, specialty coffee hadn't really taken off in New Zealand but there was something about it that captured me: the specificity, the attention to quality, the way every minute detail can so drastically affect the flavour profile, while at its core it's just one ingredient. My curiosity has always led me to the most interesting places, and once I got a taste for coffee I went all in. Coffee opened up the world for me: I got to compete and represent New Zealand on the world stage after winning the New Zealand Barista Championship in 2016 and the New Zealand Latte Art Championship in 2013 and 2015.

After that, I was at a bit of a loss. What now? I'd achieved my biggest goal at the time, and I didn't know who I was besides a person who *loved* coffee.

On the side I'd been cooking and sharing on social media the dishes I was creating and experimenting with. Mostly this was Chinese food. That was when I created Da Lin ('dial in'), to dial in to my 'Chineseness' and really understand that part of myself.

Da Lin was a pop-up concept where I'd create things like tofu and century egg purée, salmon roe on steamed salmon, and my version of char siu (Chinese barbecue pork). Using the ingredients available around me, I was drawing on my own experience and influences to assimilate Chinese food into my environment without even knowing it.

I wasn't creating the sort of dishes you'd see in a Cantonese restaurant — it was different. It felt exciting and new, while still paying homage to my family, and to the cuisine's place of origin. Ultimately, my food reflects who I am: this mish-mash of everywhere and everything I've experienced.

It's taken me a long time to understand the value of the food I grew up with. Cooking and experimenting with its flavours feels like a retaliation against the negativity I felt about my cultural identity when I was younger; it feels like a political moment where I can go: 'Hey, this food *is* worthy of attention.' My journey of developing as a cook, and approaching Chinese food in an unconventional way (my way), has made me really appreciate the fact that being 'Chinese' exists on a spectrum — everyone has their own way of doing it.

2020 was a big year for me. I moved back to New Zealand from Melbourne, came out to my family as gay, and managed to go viral for re-plating room-service food while stuck in hotel quarantine! Bored out of my mind, I'd lather myself in luxury skincare, diffuse aromatherapy scents throughout the room, and transform the cardboard-box dishes into plates that looked like they came out of a fine-dining restaurant. I was *living*, baby.

The story went everywhere, from overseas news outlets to the Instagram feed of our then prime minister, Jacinda Ardern. I loved how it injected a bit of joy into people's lives during what felt like a pretty joyless time — it was a great creative escape, but it also felt good that I was able to spread that positivity. That's been my main motivator through everything, including the very thing that got me onto this page, and into your home — winning *MasterChef NZ*.

MasterChef felt like a way to do what I loved best: telling and celebrating diverse food stories. It was, and remains, one of the hardest things I've ever done — physically and mentally. I didn't just want to cook well, but embody my absolute truth, with a generous openness about being Chinese and queer. I know it sounds like a cliché, but I wanted to be the kind of person I wished I had seen on my screen growing up; the representation that may have made things just a little bit easier for younger Sam. (I feel like younger Sam would be pretty happy with where I've ended up.)

The show made me a more confident cook, that's for sure, and pushed me out of my comfort zone more times than not. But, more than anything, it gave me an avenue through which to fully embrace my identity, to cook food that is meaningful to me, and to spread that to others.

This book is a small glimpse into my life: the food I want to eat, the things I want to cook for my friends and family. Food is made to be enjoyed. Make the dishes in this book that you'd want to eat, get some rice on the table, and invite loved ones over to share in it all.

That's why I wrote this book.

Please — feast!

Sam Low

'Chineseness'

The first time I visited China, as a young boy, my parents took me to their hometown, Zhongshan, in Guangdong, southern China.

We went to a huge restaurant owned by someone in my extended family — and when I say huge, I mean it sat about 600 people. It was two storeys high, and everyone working there wore earpieces so they could communicate. *Pure chaos but controlled.* There were these gigantic fish tanks filled with water snakes, water bugs, varieties of fish and lobsters. We were served an elaborate banquet with dishes that featured offal and insects: think huhu grub omelettes and tough pigeons. These were the foods Zhongshan was known for. And, to be honest, I didn't enjoy any of it.

You could spend a lifetime trying to understand Chinese gastronomy and you'd only scratch the surface. *It's complicated.* There are over 20 provinces in China, each with its own regional specialty fare. And they are huge! I mean, Sichuan alone is bigger than France. So you cannot begin to imagine the entire Chinese culinary landscape. And that's before you even count all the diasporic food that has emerged from Chinese emigration to other countries.

In most rural towns and a lot of city suburbs in Aotearoa New Zealand you'll find a fish and chip shop run by Chinese immigrants. These places are where a lot of us had our first experience of Chinese food. The shops have those PVC butcher strips or string-beaded curtains at the entrance, hand-written signs, and a distinctive smell of old oil.

Above the counter, the menu on the wall will be divided in two: one side has chips by the scoopful, spring rolls, fish and sausages fried in batter. The other side offers chow mein (fried noodles), fried rice and sweet corn soup.

These are all examples of a certain type of Cantonese food that developed as communities immigrated to the West from that part of China. The US is home to some of the oldest Chinatowns — a way of assimilating themselves and making money. That's how dishes like chop suey (a stir-fry with gravy) and sweet-and-sour pork came into the world. Chinese, but adapted to the place — a concept I can definitely identify with.

Though I mostly grew up eating Cantonese food, I started to explore the diversity of regional Chinese cuisine as it seeped into New Zealand mainstream with the growth of Chinese migration. I remember eating at a Hunanese restaurant in Auckland's Dominion Road (which wasn't popular the way it is now). The dishes we ordered were so different: cold rice-wine-marinated duck, Yunnan ham steamed on tofu with fresh peas, dried shrimp on vegetables. Everything tasted different to what I was used to, even though the techniques — steaming, curing, dehydrating — were typical to Chinese cuisine.

One of my other favourite restaurants on Dominion Road, JadeTown, serves Uyghur cuisine. Lamb with cumin is a classic combination, but it's rare to find lamb dishes in Cantonese fare. At JadeTown, chilli and cumin are the prominent flavour profiles, betraying influence from the north-bordering countries of China, like Mongolia. They also serve fermented and pickled ingredients from Russia. You end up eating things like rice cooked in carrot broth with a side of fermented pickled cabbage and glass noodles. To me, this speaks volumes about how varied Chinese cuisine is.

Being exposed to more types of Chinese food felt so exciting; it really made me think about Chinese cuisine having a bigger story, and all the interesting things you could do with it. It's crazy how different these styles of Chinese food can taste and look, and yet they're all still recognisable to us as being 'Chinese'.

Besides Cantonese food, Sichuan cuisine has probably had the most impact on the way I cook, and the recipes in this book. It's polarisingly different to Cantonese fare: ladled with chilli oil, spicier, with that numbing mala flavour that is unique to the region. You'll find it in some of the dishes I make, combining ingredients that normally wouldn't be found together.

At the end of the day, though, I can't help but go back to the type of Chinese eating I know. And anyone who knows me knows that is yum cha. I'm constantly inviting my friends out for yum cha; it's one of my favourite ways of eating — my one true love. It's big and elaborate and grand! Yum cha is an affordable way to sample so many textures and flavours shared among a group of people as the lazy susan, heaving with small dishes in bamboo steamers and on white plates, goes round and round.

Washed down with hot tea, yum cha is the ultimate form of brunch. What I really love is the detail and precision that go into every dim sum. It requires skill and time to produce these perfect morsels, and the texture of the rice-flour wrappers is not easy to master. And, yet, you can get a serving of xiaolongbao or har gao for under $10. Damn, it's amazing.

My understanding of Chinese food — and the way I cook it — is going to keep evolving because there's just so much to discover. This means the potential for 'future me' to grow and learn is limitless . . . and I love that for him.

Queer Food

I had my first crush on a boy when I was eight. I still remember that his name was Afoa. I didn't know what it was at the time, but I'd bring little gifts to him, like adventure playing cards, food snacks or random toys from inside Kinder Surprises. It was very cute now that I think about it.

It wasn't until intermediate that I met someone who was openly gay — a fellow student. It was the first time I was able to put a word to that feeling — 'gay' — and understand that that was what I was too. But I thought maybe it was temporary. Everyone went through that phase at some stage, right?

Either way, I repressed it — partly, I think, because it was so hard growing up in a conservative household, and within a conservative culture. There wasn't a whole lot of LGBT representation in Fijian or even New Zealand media when I was younger, which meant that we never had much exposure to that 'world'. That community consisted of other people, not people like me. That was one reason I fell so deeply in love with food and hospitality — it gave me a distraction from a part of my life that I chose not to explore.

That was until I moved overseas. I moved to Melbourne in 2014, aged 22, and being in a new city with a large queer community allowed me to explore that side of my identity. It felt good — really good. But in the back of my mind I worried about what my friends and family would think.

At 24 I decided to come out to my best friends in New Zealand via a video call. Thankfully, they were all really accepting. Being transparent with my closest community was really important validation for me, because part of me still felt guilty about the whole thing. There was a bit of shame attached, because of my upbringing.

Coming out to my parents years later, after moving back to New Zealand in 2020, opened up a whole new pathway to learning about how my queerness influenced the way I think about food.

When I say the food I cook is queer, I don't mean it's filled with rainbow-coloured food dye or edible glitter, but that what I put on the plate falls outside of the box; it's outside society's norms. I was privileged to show this during my journey on MasterChef, where the food I cooked during challenges tended towards unique flavour combinations — things that may have seemed a little weird, or 'wrong' — like the seafood dessert I put up in the finale, which used kombu ice cream paired with nori meringue, topped with jasmine granita, steamed matcha cake and compressed fruits.

I learned recently that queerness played a significant part in the publication of

Western cookbooks published in the aftermath of World War II. Many of the cookbooks around that time were published by major sugar and flour companies in order to sell their products. Surprisingly enough, a lot of these were written by closeted queer men, their sexuality never publicly revealed for fear of affecting book sales. And as we know, today the food media is dominated by women and queer men — such as James Beard, the namesake of the biggest food media awards in the US.

Coming out to my parents was pivotal to a shift in the way I approach life and what I do. It triggered a realisation that because I don't fit a lot of societal boxes anyway, I should question every decision I make, to be sure I'm not simply conforming to society's expectations. Even while creating this book, I've been careful with how the imagery has been presented. I didn't want things to come across as too feminine or too masculine, and I wanted to make sure I wasn't dressing up photos in a quest for 'oriental' imagery to feed into a certain 'Chinese' story or narrative. Essentially, it's made me think: is what I'm doing from my own genuine, personal beliefs, or does it stem from societal expectations?

Embracing my queerness has had such a positive effect on my cooking. It's given me the freedom of knowing there are no rules or boundaries I have to play along with; I don't have to adhere to the traditional canon or methodology of doing anything. It's about being respectful, but creating new, innovative pairings where I can, and about being bold.

My existence, and being open about who I am, is already pushing boundaries — and my food should reflect that. It should be an honest reflection of me. And I think it finally is. I'm improvising and adapting — crafting my own food culture and identity on a journey of discovery with the people and places around me.

Kitchen Equipment

There are a few basic items of cooking equipment I encourage people to invest in; and as someone who has often been temporarily based overseas, or living in rentals with housemates, I recognise the desire to commit to high-quality (and therefore usually expensive) equipment for the kitchen. With that in mind, I have curated a list of kitchen essentials that won't break the bank — no one needs a jet-powered wok burner.

Many kitchens are fitted with ceramic cooktops, induction or electric heating elements rather than gas, and certain equipment, such as woks, might not be suitable. That's totally okay, I have been there and you can still achieve well-executed Chinese food that even the toughest of Chinese aunties would happily devour.

Here are the things I recommend you have in your kitchen:

A wok and/or slightly deeper fry pans with lids: Woks come in many different types and forms, ranging from flat-base, non-stick types to carbon steel, rounded-base woks. Many will tell you that you need a great wok to make great-tasting Chinese food, but I disagree. I'm not trying to mimic what my parents cooked on their gas hob in the tool shed (where they set up a second kitchen for more intense cooking). Nor am I trying to replicate the complicated dishes made in Chinese restaurants where foods kiss the gas flames while being flipped up and out of a wok to develop that distinctive smoky flavour known as 'Wok Hei' (breath of the wok).

You just want a wok or a pan big enough to retain the heat and to fit a large volume of foods before they wilt down, such as leafy greens. A lid is important as it allows you to steam the food, thus reducing the cooking time. I often use my main pan to deep-fry, shallow-fry, stir-fry, pan-fry and simmer. I recommend getting pans with a bit of weight for heat retention and a couple of sizes — 20 cm and 30 cm (8 in and 12 in) diameter. With woks get one that is about 30–40 cm (12–16 in) diameter at the top, and for most cooktops you're looking for a heavier wok. However, if you have a powerful gas burner, a lighter, thinner wok is ideal for wok-flipping.

Pots with lids: I often boil, simmer and steam foods, soups and broths and this is where varied sized pots come in handy. I will always have at least three sizes: a small 1 litre (35 fl oz) pot for sauces and reheating or cooking small volumes of food; a medium 3–4 litre (105–140 fl oz) pot for the majority of tasks, such as boiling dumplings, making stews or blanching vegetables; and a larger 6–8 litre (210–280 fl oz) pot with a heavy base for making broths and soups for larger parties and/or for steaming by topping with a steamer basket.

Steamer baskets: Initially, it may look intimidating but once you get used to a steamer basket, you'll find it's such a great way to create healthy home-cooked meals without much fuss. I highly recommend buying lidded bamboo steamer baskets, as these allow for more of a dry steam — the steel steamers with glass lids can create more condensation and result in unwanted liquid in your dish. Find a size that would fit inside your largest pot or wok and buy at least two so you can stack them, allowing for multiple components — such as fish and eggs — to be cooked at the same time.

Electric kettle: You'll find that a bunch of the recipes in the book require hot water to quickly blanch ingredients, soak dry ingredients or rinse impurities off meat. This is where a kettle will save you so much time — and cleaning — so you don't have to boil a pot of water every time.

Microwave: I grew up using microwaves and to be honest I don't think I can live without one, it's such a versatile appliance. A few of the recipes in the book will benefit from or require the use of a microwave to help you save time, including creating simple syrups, reheating sauces, cooking fish, making cakes and defrosting things. I also use it on a low heat setting to bring ingredients such as butter and cream cheese to room temperature.

Stainless steel mixing bowls: You can never have too many of these. Every time I cook I'll use four to five of them and they are usually the first thing I pull out when setting up. I will always use one for waste, so I don't need to run to the bin every time I need to discard something. Get different sizes — 1 litre (35 fl oz) , 2 litre (70 fl oz) and 4 litre (140 fl oz) is a good starting set — you'll be so grateful you did.

Wooden chopsticks: These are not just for eating with but also to cook with. They're the ideal implement for moving ingredients around in a pan or wok, and in pots to prevent food from sticking. The larger and longer ones are especially designed for cooking, however the standard ones will do the trick just fine.

Rice cooker: I have grown up using a rice cooker, it's just something I've always had. You can find these everywhere now at a super-affordable price. They're really easy to use and once you figure out your ratios of rice to water you'll have perfectly cooked rice every single time.

Chinese cleaver, Chinese chef's knife and/or Tou (a Chinese meat and vegetable knife): These are a range of knives that, once you get the hang of them, will become your go-to knives for everything from cutting raw fish to pork crackling to cakes. They are designed to be extremely versatile and are made with a decent-sized flat side of the blade for scooping chopped ingredients and smacking things like garlic and ginger. I just use cheaper knives that are normally found in Asian grocers. The secret is to keep them sharp, so I use one of those sliding knife sharpeners every week to keep them at a consistent sharpness. Whetstones are also recommended if you know how to use them well.

Stack of small bowls: These are not only great for individual servings of rice, but a handy way to set up all your prepped ingredients before starting to cook them in a wok/pan. In this kind of cooking, ingredients don't take much time to cook, so you need everything prepped and close by, ready to throw into the wok/pan.

Large wooden chopping board: A large, sturdy wooden chopping board, approx. 40–50 cm (16–20 in), is worth the investment. They make food prep so much more enjoyable and if you're not cooking for too many there'll be space on it for all your different prepped ingredients rather than needing to transfer everything into small bowls — less washing up. I will also use smaller wooden or plastic boards placed on top of the large wooden board for things like meats, seafood or things I don't want to contaminate the large board.

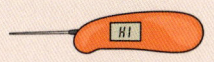

Thermometer: This is handy for measuring the temperature of oil for frying. I started off using the probe types and have now invested in a laser gun type (it's not too expensive) to check when the oil or fry pan is at the perfect cooking temperature.

Spatulas: Multiple spatulas made of different materials will always have their uses. In pretty much every recipe I will use a wooden and a rubber spatula, the wooden one to move food around the wok/pan and the rubber one to scrape the sauces and gravy around and into the serving dish. Spatulas are cheap so having a few means you won't need to wash them all the time.

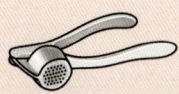

Garlic crusher: Not only will you be eliminating the need to finely chop garlic, leaving your chopping board with an intense garlic smell, you'll find that you'll be less annoyed about preparing garlic once you have a garlic press. Plus, perhaps surprisingly, it will make your garlic go further! By crushing the garlic and not chopping it, you will release more oils and aromatics, making it go further by fully utilising its flavour potential.

Serveware: Start collecting a mix of large and smaller plates, platters and bowls to ensure you can properly serve food to the table, including utensils such as serving spoons, small tongs and ladles. Also think about having the appropriate dishes for things that are cooked in their serving vessel — for example plates large enough to fit a whole fish from the steamer basket, or dishes deep enough to steam a batch of eggs in.

Jars: I love having spare jars on hand for when I want to make a batch of something special such as chilli oils or sauces to store in the fridge. Jars will keep your foods fresher for longer and give your food that home-made feel, which is such a lovely sensation. Home-made condiments in jars also make incredible gifts, with so much care and sentiment attached.

Masking tape and a marker: A marker and masking tape in your kitchen drawer is super handy for creating instant labels for things like home-made sauces and leftovers. It's also a great way to label seasonings/spices in your pantry, and it'll make you feel like you're in a professional kitchen.

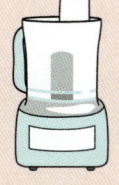

Food processor: As appliances advance and with different versions popping up left and right, it should be easy to find a processor to suit your needs, whether it be large and industrial-strength or compact and more affordable. They are super handy for chopping and blending high volumes of ingredients such as ginger and garlic.

Cooking Techniques

Preparation

Cutting: Knowing Chinese cuts is fundamental to understanding how Chinese cuisine is consumed. Most dishes will be consumed using chopsticks, therefore most things need to be cut to a suitable size — not too small or too big. Cutting ingredients into uniform sizes will also mean that the ingredients will cook evenly. If an ingredient is cut into large chunks, usually it will be cooked until it is softened to a point where you can break it easily with chopsticks.

There are many different types of cuts for vegetables. The best way to think about it is to consider the ingredient and the cooking time required for it to be at its ideal texture. For example, in a stir-fry a hard carrot would be cut thinner than a capsicum because a capsicum is softer than a carrot and will reach its ideal texture quicker. In terms of length and width, both would be cut similarly but their thickness would be different. For most of my recipes I will give suggestions on the ideal size for ingredients to be cut into and many of them are visible in the recipe photos too. Have a look, play around using trial and error and find what's best for your personal preference.

A handy hint for slicing things that can be difficult to cut, such as raw meats and fish, is to freeze the ingredient for about an hour before slicing. This will stiffen it enough to help you achieve a more even cut.

Smacking: A common technique used on garlic cloves, ginger pieces, certain spices and spring onion whites to break open the ingredient and release its flavours before cooking. It's mostly done with the side of a Chinese-style knife. In certain recipes, some other vegetables will benefit from this preparation technique, such as the cucumbers in my Smashed Cucumber Salad (see page 43). Smashing the cucumber pieces creates crevices to hold more sauce and seasoning.

Marinating: There are two common types of marination in Chinese cooking. One is a simple application of aromatic ingredients to remove or reduce the intense smell of raw ingredients such as fish or meat (expelling its fishiness or gaminess). Often this involves using rice wine, ginger and white pepper. The second type of marination is called 'velveting', where the cut ingredients (usually a protein) are mixed with a starch (often cornflour), seasoning and rice wine — sometimes water and/or baking soda are also used. This process will cause the fibres in the protein to start to break down and therefore tenderise it. It's usually done for stir-fries, to give you a more tender bite.

Cooking

Blanching: This technique involves using hot water on vegetables and meat for different reasons. To remove the raw 'green' flavour from vegetables and to allow for a quicker cook time, I will often use a kettle of boiled water to either soak or pour over the vegetables before their second cook. In the Simple Dry-fry Green Beans recipe (see page 99), the beans are blanched in hot water and drained before the stir-fry stage. Chunks of meat are commonly rinsed or blanched before using them in broths to remove any impurities from the meat, such as blood, to allow for a clearer broth.

Stir-frying: A quick and perhaps the most common method of cooking in Chinese households, stir-frying is a great way to preserve the natural qualities of each ingredient added. For vegetables, its benefits are to retain their textures and nutritional value and for meats the beautiful tenderness and succulence. It's important to have all your ingredients prepped and near your wok/pan station before you start cooking, as the cook time is usually very short between the addition of ingredients. Ensure your pan/wok is hot before use to prevent sticking and allow for the caramelisation of the ingredients, and to reduce the amount of steaming and having your vegetables seep out all their waters.

Steaming: This is one of the oldest Chinese methods of cooking and is one of my favourites. It showcases the purest flavours from the ingredients, such as the delicate flavours of fish or eggs. I highly recommend using a bamboo steamer; however, you can also use a large pot or wok with a trivet placed in the middle above the level of the water. Place the plate of food on the trivet, cover it with a lid and steam away.

Deep-frying: Though it's not a cooking technique I use often, I will sometimes deep-fry on a special occasion or if I want to impress guests. Deep-frying may be used for the full cooking process, while in other recipes, such as with eggplant or fried squid, it's just used for the first stage of cooking and then the food is finished off in a sauce or a stir-fry. I don't have a deep-fryer so I just use a deeper pan or wok to fry, and if the oil doesn't have too much in the way of sediment after use I'll keep it in a jar to reuse within a week or so.

Building Your Chinese Pantry

I'm often asked by peers why their food always seems to taste the same, regardless of what they cook. 'Well,' I ask back, 'how well stocked is your pantry? And are you using the same seasonings and spices across different dishes?' The answer is usually yes.

In my opinion, building a comprehensive pantry in your kitchen is perhaps the most important thing to get right. It's the easiest way to make sure your fresh produce ends up tasting delicious and full of flavour, even with the most mundane ingredients.

The pantry ingredients listed here might seem large or intimidating; however, I promise it's not as scary as you think. I've sorted these suggested pantries into three tiers, with Tier One reflecting the most basic and accessible ingredients, Tier Two the next step up, which includes goods you can find in a well-stocked Western supermarket, and Tier Three featuring speciality items you might only see at an Asian grocer. Even if you stick to Tier One, you'll find you'll be able to make most of the dishes in this book — in fact you'll most likely have most of these at home already.

I always encourage people to try new or different ingredients often, and not just experimenting with a new spice or seasoning, but even trying a different brand of the same staple so you can slowly curate your own ideal pantry. This is something I do constantly.

Over the years, I have moved and lived overseas multiple times, so I'm familiar with building a pantry from scratch. To help you on your journey, I have a few tips that might be helpful to ensure your cooking experience is as stress-free as possible:

- Buy a bunch of small (250 ml/9 fl oz) and medium (500 ml/17 fl oz) airtight, transparent and stackable containers to store spices and seasoning. Label them, with a marker or on masking tape. I recommend buying about 20–30 to start.

- I store high-use liquids, such as rice wine, soy sauce and cooking oil, in easy-to-use squeezy bottles. This means you can bulk-buy large bottles of them and then decant them into your squeezy bottles as you need. This also has the advantage of allowing you to keep the majority of your oils out of the light, which can make oils go rancid.

- Have your higher-use seasonings and spices within close reach, and the lesser-used ingredients in the back so you're not constantly moving and restacking your spice containers. Try grouping your similar spices together — for example, cloves, star anise and cassia.

Pantry Staples Tier One

This is a list of the pantry staples I use to cook almost every meal at home. It contains a good range of seasoning and spices to create complex, balanced flavours — and, the best part is, it's super accessible to most. These ingredients are easily found in any supermarket, even those without a dedicated international aisle, and are must-haves in your pantry.

They are ordered by frequency of use in my own pantry, from most to least used.

Seasoning:

Salt: Table salt is the most common type used in Chinese households, both because of how affordable it is, but also because it's used to make things salty, rather than as a finishing salt or as a textural component, as might be the case in other cuisines.

Sugar: White sugar is the default in Chinese cuisine. Similar to salt, it is used purely to add sweetness rather than develop flavour (unless stated otherwise for certain recipes).

Dark soy sauce: Mostly used to add colour to a dish and a slight aromatic nuance of deep-rich earthy tones.

Light soy sauce: This is commonly used to add saltiness and a touch of complex savouriness to dishes. More often than not, the more expensive the soy, the more complex its flavour, largely due to the fermentation process. I often have a range of different soy sauces in my pantry, each with a different complexity to suit the contrasting flavour outcomes I want to achieve.

White pepper powder: I believe this is one of the most underutilised spices in the West but it's such an important way to add complexity to Chinese food. The intensely perfumed floral and earthy notes make this a powerful spice, and a little goes a long way. It's commonly used to remove other intense flavours from raw ingredients, such as removing the fishiness from fish, or the flavour of game from red meats.

Black peppercorns: Though not commonly used in Chinese cooking, I have found black peppercorns can add a lovely spice kick instead of chilli in certain dishes such as stir-fry. Whole peppercorns are great in stews or broth to add depth of flavour.

Rice wine: Rice wine is one of the most crucial ingredients to have in a Chinese pantry and is often used for marinades and to enhance the flavours of meat. The ones I use the most are Shaoxing rice wines, which come from the eastern region of China, where they are known for their amber-coloured rice wines. These wines come in a range of prices, fermentation ages and, again, flavour complexities. I often have three different types on hand and swap them out depending on how I want to use them. These are not designed for drinking!

Rice wine vinegar: A lightly acidic vinegar used mostly as a vinaigrette or a quick pickle solution to add acidity to dishes, this has a slightly rich flavour of sweet rice, which makes it more exciting than white vinegar.

Black vinegar: AKA Chinkiang or brown rice vinegar, this is a popular vinegar that originated in the Zhenjiang, an eastern province of China. Made from fermented glutinous rice, it gives food a deep, complex flavour, almost akin to molasses, and a tame acidity.

White vinegar and apple cider vinegar: These staples add acidity to dishes that don't need more colour or extra layers of complexity and are used purely to amp up the vibrancy of a dish.

Chicken bouillon powder/stock powder: Instead of using pure MSG, I often use chicken bouillon powder to add complexity and savouriness to a dish. It is usually made with chicken essence (dehydrated chicken stock) and a combination of MSG and salt. I will buy these in large packets at my local Asian grocer. The more expensive, the higher the chicken essence percentage. A little goes a long way, so it's worth the investment.

Modern Chinese

Spices:

Ground cumin: When ground the potency of cumin is heightened, creating such an intoxicating, addictive smell. It's excellent sprinkled over grilled meats, especially lamb, or fried chicken.

Cloves: A spice from the flowering bud of an evergreen tree, cloves have a flavour reminiscent of warm spices such as nutmeg or cinnamon. Cloves are used in many Chinese medicine applications and are also a key component of five-spice powder. Cloves are used in broths and in stews to infuse with meats, especially red meat.

Onion powder: This is made by dehydrating and grinding onion into a fine powder for an intense flavour. Great in marinades or to add onion flavour without the liquid components of pieces of onion.

Chilli flakes: Different types of dried chilli provide different levels of intensity in heat and spiciness and can potentially add nuanced flavour characteristics. I like the milder dried chilli flakes made from the 'facing heaven chilli pepper', a cone-shaped mild chilli with citrus notes. With this chilli I can add more to a dish if I feel like it can benefit from it, rather than having to control its use because of its heat level. I recommend trying different types and brands to find your favourite.

Five-spice powder: This blend of five or more spices makes a complex and fragrant addition to dishes, adding complexity and warmth. Common components of five-spice powder are star anise, cloves, fennel seeds, Sichuan peppercorns and cinnamon or cassia. I like five-spice blends that contain ground dried citrus peels, such as tangerine, as it results in a more unique and interesting flavour.

Star anise: Mostly found in its dried state, star anise is a star-shaped fruit known for its aniseed flavour, similar to liquorice or fennel, and is commonly used in five-spice powder. Used in stews or broths to add a lightness and brightness in aroma.

Cumin seeds: One of my favourite spices, because of its vibrancy and vegetal fresh notes. Commonly used in northern Chinese cuisine because of the influences of its neighbouring territories, such as Mongolia and the Middle East.

Garlic powder: Garlic is dehydrated and pulverised into an intensely flavoured powder. This works well in a dry spice blend to sprinkle over fried foods, or to use in marinades to avoid having bits of garlic in the food, for example when marinating skewers for barbecuing.

Other staples:

Fresh ginger: Another one of the most versatile and important ingredients in Chinese cooking, ginger is used in both sweet and savoury dishes. It has healing properties and a distinctive acidity, which makes this ingredient one of my favourites. I almost never peel ginger as I don't think it makes a huge difference. However, if you do choose to peel it, using a teaspoon to scrape away the skin is the best way to go.

Fresh garlic: One of the most crucial ingredients in Chinese cooking, garlic is in almost every savoury recipe in this book. If I know I am doing a large banquet or making sauces or dishes that require a lot of garlic, I often buy the packs of peeled garlic to make life a little easier — take heed if you hate peeling it too. If you have time, you can peel a bunch of garlic cloves ahead of time and store them in the fridge — they last up to a week this way.

Cooking oil (canola, vegetable): In most cases I use canola or high-temperature cooking oil such as vegetable or rapeseed. These are neutral in flavour and work well as a blank canvas to infuse flavours into, for example when making chilli oil (see page 192).

Spring onion: I use this ingredient often in my recipes because it's almost like an elevated onion, with parts for cooking and parts for garnishing. You'll see in many of the recipes I suggest you separate the whites and greens to use at different times. If you keep spring onions in a jug of water — like a vase of flowers — they'll last for a good while on your counter. Or you can keep the greens and whites separate and store them in a sealable bag to prolong their shelf life. If you don't have any handy you may substitute regular onion.

Cornflour: Cornflower is excellent to coat food for frying, as it creates a light outer coating that's crisp and delicate. It's also an excellent thickening agent, especially when mixed with an equal quantity of water — making what's known as a slurry. If you don't have cornflour to hand you can also create a slurry using tapioca or potato starch.

Brown onion: This pantry staple is often used in combination with garlic and ginger — the Asian trinity — to create complex and fragrant stir-fries or stews. Onions add a ton of sweetness to dishes and, when just cooked through, they also add a nice crunch.

Building Your Chinese Pantry

Pantry Staples Tier Two

This section includes some speciality Chinese ingredients that will sometimes require a quick trip to your local Asian grocer. The ingredients here are not easily substituted with anything else as they have very specific flavours and characteristics to make the dishes they're used in more unique.

A trip to the Asian grocer is a good opportunity to explore the various brands and iterations of the same products, just like you might for olive oil or mayonnaise, to help you to find your favourite. Trying different brands of soy sauce or rice wine can show you how changing the quality of the seasoning makes a huge difference a dish rather than adding new or different ingredients.

Several of the ingredients in Tier Two and Tier Three are ones that are super complex and created using the magic of fermentation, preservation, drying and/or curing. Like the complex ingredients found in other cultures — such as aged cheeses, cured meats or pickled vegetables — these ingredients can help to develop delicious umami (savoury) flavours in a dish.

Toasted sesame oil: The oil extracted from toasted sesame seeds is incredibly aromatic, with a deep nutty and fragrant aroma. Generally used as a finishing oil to drizzle over foods such as stir-fries or noodles, it's added just before a dish is almost cooked. Go for a higher-quality one because a little goes a long way and it's worth the investment. I tend to buy smaller bottles, because it tastes best when freshly opened.

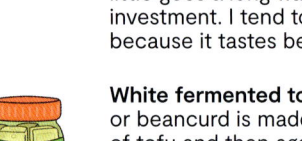

White fermented tofu: Fermented tofu or beancurd is made by drying cubes of tofu and then ageing them in a salt brine until the tofu has a blue cheese-like consistency and a deliciously funky flavour. Used as a side dish or in dishes to add a depth of savouriness.

Oyster sauce: A thick, rich savoury sauce made with a combination of oyster extract, salt, sugar, water and a thickening agent. Vegetarian versions of oyster sauce are made with mushroom extract, making it a great vegan alternative. The general rule of thumb is that the higher the oyster extract percentage, the higher quality the product.

Bay leaves: Bay leaves are commonly used in several cuisines, including Chinese, added to broths or stews for more spice complexity. Bay also helps reduce the flavour of gaminess from meats in the dish. Mild and gentle in flavour.

Dried shiitake mushrooms: These dried fungi are concentrated and packed with umami. They are a key ingredient used across many Chinese regions to add a depth of savouriness to dishes. After rehydration, the mushrooms become soft and easy to chop and the soaking water makes a great mushroom stock to add to broths or stews.

Dried chillis (whole): Different types of chillis will provide different flavours and heat levels. I always prefer milder ones so I can build more or less flavour in a dish without worrying about making it too spicy. Whole chillis are great in stews or toasted in oil and then removed to aromatise the oil before cooking. You can also grind whole dried chillis using a mortar and pestle or in a food processor until coarsely ground into chilli flakes.

Cassia bark (Chinese cinnamon): A type of cinnamon that is less sharp and sweet smelling than common cinnamon. The bark is darker and thicker, with a deep spice aroma. Great used in small quantities for stews and broths. You may substitute this with the more commonly found cinnamon sticks.

Fermented chilli paste (doubanjiang): A Chinese fermented chilli paste that is made with fermented broad beans, soybeans, chilli and garlic. It's a key flavouring ingredient for Sichuan cuisine and can be used in many applications, including sauces, stews and stir-fries, adding a deep salty, spicy and savoury taste.

Red fermented tofu: This consists of cubes of tofu or beancurd dried and then fermented in brine, made with red rice yeast, which adds a red colour and unique flavour to the tofu. Often used in stews or meat marinades.

Black fermented soy bean: Aka black bean, this is made by salting and fermenting soybeans until they are black and savoury in flavour. This umami bomb of a seasoning is used to season gravies or stir-fries, adding a salty and slightly sweet bitter pop to a dish.

Modern Chinese

Hoisin: This sweet and salty Cantonese-style sauce is made from fermented soybean paste and seasoned with five-spice powder, sugar and, depending on the manufacturing region, a variety of other ingredients. Great to use in stir-fries, stews and dips.

Chilli oil: This is my favourite condiment in my pantry. A good chilli oil will lift any meal and bring it to another level, especially if it contains other aromatics to uplift its complexities. I highly recommend making a batch of your own and have created a few recipe variations for you to try (see page 192–195). Once you start you won't go back to store-bought and you can experiment over time, adding or removing ingredients to make your own personal ultimate chilli oil.

Sichuan peppercorns: Despite the name, there are no peppercorns involved here. This unique spice is the husk of prickly ash shrubs that are related to the citrus family, which explains the floral and vibrant nature of this spice. These are a key ingredient in Sichuan cuisine, often cooked with chilli to create the flavour 'Ma La', meaning numbing and spicy. When used in the right amounts it will elevate a dish and bring sweetness and complexity to a meal. I tend to buy and store different versions of this spice: ground into a powder, whole, and in an oil form to use to finish dishes.

Pantry Staples Tier Three

Here, we are getting more into the 'sometimes' category — well, for me, anyway. These are ingredients I keep in the pantry or freezer and use on occasion to mix things up, especially for special occasions or gatherings.

Century egg: A unique Chinese delicacy made by fermenting duck eggs in salt, ash, clay, quicklime and rice husks. The egg ferments for months until it becomes a dark amber colour. The egg whites and yolk become grey and soft and the resulting flavour is reminiscent of liver paté.

Dried goji berries: A small dried red berry that is used in Chinese cooking to add a slight hint of sweetness to broths or teas. It's also well-known for its healing properties and health benefits. I would generally throw in a couple of spoons of these into a broth for exactly those reasons.

Dried red dates: Dried dates add a natural sweetness and more nutrients to broths or soups. I often use dates in combination with goji berries for a beautiful complex sweetness that you can't get with sugar. You can find different types of dried dates and I suggest trying different types and brands to find the ones you like.

Dried shrimp/prawns: Dried shrimp or prawns also come in a variety of sizes. Thin and tiny dried shrimp are used directly — just add them to stir-fries or broths. However, the larger types need to be reconstituted and used along with their soaking liquid to extract the maximum flavour. For the larger dried prawns, I would store them in an airtight bag in the freezer to maintain their flavour.

Chinese dried sausage (lap cheong): This is one of my favourite Chinese ingredients. There are many types of Chinese dried sausage and they can be used in so many different ways. The version I grew up with are the sweet Cantonese types that are relatively thin and long and made with pork, pork fat, spices and rose wine (a sweet fragrant rice wine). They are packed full of flavour. Slice them and add them to stir-fried rice dishes and broths.

Wood ear fungus (black fungus): A black, ear-shaped wild fungus, this has minimal flavour, but it has a unique crisp texture which makes it very popular in Chinese cooking. It's also popular for its health properties. These are commonly found in the dried goods section of an Asian grocer and must be reconstituted before using, but the soaking liquid is not used.

Dehydrated scallops: Dried scallops are used to flavour broths, stocks and sauces, adding a rich, sweet and savoury seafood flavour. They must be reconstituted before use by soaking in water until softened. Make sure to use the soaking liquid too, as that will contain a lot of the flavour. They come in various sizes and qualities. More often than not, the larger the scallops the more expensive they are. I like to store my dried scallops in the freezer in an airtight bag so they don't lose their flavour intensity.

Building Your Chinese Pantry

Chinese black cardamom (tsaoko): This is currently one of my favourite spices. Very different to green cardamom, the black cardamom pod is much larger and has a really distinctive smoky, peppery and warming smell. Use in small amounts (just one or two) in braises, stews or broths to add a level of aromatic complexity. The pods must be crushed or smacked open using the side of a cleaver before use to release the flavour from the seeds within.

Preserved olive vegetable: This savoury jar of goodness is one of my favourite condiments. It's made from a combination of preserved Chinese olives, mustard leaves, salt and oil and can be used straight out of the jar on noodles or rice, or to add a lovely depth of flavour to stir-fries. There tend to be a few pits from the olives in the jars so be careful not to bite into them.

Sichuan pepper oil: This is made by infusing neutral oil with Sichuan pepper, creating an intensely aromatic oil with the flavour of the peppercorn without the woody bits. The oil has a lovely citrusy and floral note with a slight tingling sensation. A little goes a long way and it's mainly used as a finishing oil to be drizzled over a dish when it's cooked.

Preserved Chinese olives (dried): Chinese olives are used very differently to olives in the West. The fruits are dried and eaten as sweet snacks, or fermented and preserved to create an intensely savoury seasoning for stir-fries, stews or sauces. Dried preserved Chinese olives are made by dehydrating olives and then simmering them in a brine made from soy sauce, salt, sugar and liquorice root. They're commonly used in stir-fries, where the olives are chopped into tiny bits before being thrown in the wok.

What is 'umami', and is MSG bad?

Sweet, salt, sour and bitter are known to be the four basic tastes. It's super important to understand them, especially when you're trying to learn how to season food to achieve flavour balance. Umami is known as the 'fifth taste' and provides a level of savouriness often referred to as 'meaty'.

When foods are aged, fermented or preserved, those processes will often result in an increase in the intensity of umami flavour. This is why we find foods that have developed that extra complexity, such as aged cured meats or parmesan, so addictively delicious.

MSG (monosodium glutamate) is a naturally occurring salt that can be used in cooking to add umami to dishes. Over the years, through negative and misinformed marketing in the West, MSG has developed a bad reputation. However, when used in the right amounts to help aid balance in seasoning and flavours, it can be a magical seasoning. Many natural foods, such as tomatoes or soy sauce, contain high amounts of MSG. If it's consumed in excess your body might object, but it's exactly the same when you consume too much sugar or salt. So don't be afraid of MSG!

Modern Chinese

How to Use this Book

Have you ever been to a restaurant where at the beginning of the meal a server arrives at your table and says, 'Have you dined with us before?' They might then proceed to tell you that, 'We do things a little differently here — everything is designed to share.'

Well, the share-plate format is a familiar concept to anyone who grew up with the Chinese way of eating, where everything, from meat to vegetables, gets plonked down in the middle of the table. Dishes are then passed around, or swivelled around on the lazy susan, to be picked at and eaten with individual servings of rice and broth. It's almost like a pick-your-own-adventure style of eating. That's been my upbringing, anyway, and is very much of the southern Cantonese tradition.

So, how do you create a meal out of the recipes from this book? Here are some loose guidelines to work with:

- If you're cooking for two to three people, you would ideally have at least one vegetable-focused dish and one protein-focused dish to share, with an optional cold appetiser or pickle. In combination with rice and broth, this creates a balanced meal, as you've got a bit of everything from carb, to vege, to meat, to the broth that's used to refresh the palate. If you don't have broth, hot tea makes a nice alternative. Pu'er, oolong and jasmine green are my picks to have at the table.

- The more people around the table, the more times you'll multiply that equation. It's a pretty simple format. In saying that, you don't need to cook two or three dishes every single time you want to put a meal together. There are a bunch of recipes in this book that contain both protein and vegetables that you can make a single serving of to go with rice, such as the Spicy Saucy Tofu (see page 104) or Braised Beef Brisket with Daikon (see page 184). Some dishes, such as Saucy Dan Dan Noodles (see page 140), or Dumplings (see pages 52–56), are designed to be eaten on their own.

- Having desserts at the end of your meal isn't very common in Chinese cuisine. Usually if you want something sweet to bookend the savoury, you'd serve a platter of fruits. I've included a collection of dessert recipes in this book that aren't typical for Chinese eating, but are a result of experimentation with Asian flavours that I really like.

- There should always be enough rice to make everyone around the table full. What's in the middle of the table is purely to season the rice. I really like this way of eating because no one is forced to eat a certain dish or is told how to have their dining experience. You're essentially creating your own degustation and encouraging intuitive eating — you can have as much, or as little, as you want.

- Season to your liking — you'll find that all the recipes in the book have quite precise measures for seasoning ingredients, but please only use these as a guide. I always encourage people to cook intuitively and season to their taste preference. If you're not a confident cook the recipe measurements are a good starting point. For most of my savoury cooking I was taught by feel, especially by my parents but also by learning to understand flavour and flavour balance. All ingredients, whether they are fresh produce or pantry items, will vary; for example the fat content of the pork, the density and moisture content of your potato or even different brands of soy sauce with varying salt levels. Taste and adjust as you go and always try your food during the cook.

- A last little tip from me: eat contrasting flavours and textures so this excites your palate. If you're having a spicy tofu, take a bite of a lightly seasoned bok choy stir-fry next, then move to plain white rice, then a sip of broth. That way, when you go back to the spicy tofu, it's like you're having it for the first time. It's my favourite way of eating.

Note on 'The Lowdown'
You'll notice there's a section on every recipe called 'The Lowdown'. This is a quick summary of how to create that recipe and the approximate time it takes to make it. I say approx. times as different skill levels will vary the time it takes to cook a dish. I always question when a cookbook says dinner in 20 minutes! More often than not it turns out to take longer than that.

   The reason why I've created 'The Lowdown' section is partly because there's nothing worse than when you're cooking from a recipe, and haven't read it all the way through, and a step in it says 'allow to marinate overnight' or 'allow to cool' which potentially could mean no dinner tonight! We've all been there, right?

   So 'The Lowdown' is me breaking it down in a short summary to avoid any unwanted surprises from creating the recipes and is also for confident cooks who want to know immediately the process required for the dish without having to read the recipe fully, especially helpful if you're revisiting the recipe and need a memory refresher.

APPS, BITES & SNACKS

CANTONESE-INSPIRED QUICK PICKLES

Growing up eating mostly southern Chinese cuisine, the forefront of my flavour memory bank was very much focused around the salt, sweet and umami (savoury) spectrum. It wasn't until I started exploring other cuisines and learning about other regional Chinese flavours that I learned that pickling and acidic accompaniments had a major role in flavour balance and often added an interesting pop of flavour to the dining table.

Ever since, I've been obsessed with having pickles or fermented acidic foods on the table to allow guests to create a more exciting eating experience. Eating a bit of savoury and salty followed by something pickled makes the meal all the more enticing.

MAKES 1.5 LITRE (52 FL OZ) JAR; SUGGESTED SERVING SIZE 50 G (1¾ OZ) PER PERSON

1 carrot (200 g/7 oz), washed well and peeled
1 telegraph cucumber (300 g/10½ oz), washed well and deseeded
1 daikon (300 g/10½ oz), washed well and peeled

Pickling liquid
2 cups rice wine vinegar
¾ cup sugar
¼ cup salt
20 g (¾ oz) fresh ginger, sliced

Prepare all the vegetables by cutting them into similar sizes. I prefer batons, approx. 5 cm x 1 cm x 0.5 cm (2 in x ½ in x ¼ in) but any shape works.

Place the veges into a sterilised, dry 1.5 litre (52 fl oz) jar or airtight container, mixing the vegetables up to make it more visually appealing and trying to keep them upright.

For the pickling liquid, bring everything to a simmer in a small saucepan. Once at a simmer, remove from the heat and stir to dissolve the sugar and salt.

Pour the hot pickling liquid over the vegetables, making sure they are all covered. If you need more liquid, make another batch following the same ratios. Allow the vegetables to cool completely.

Cover and store in the fridge.

They can be consumed immediately but are best after a day stored in the fridge and will keep for up to 2 weeks. Always use a clean utensil when handling to prevent spoilage.

THE LOWDOWN
Clean and cut the vegetables and place in a sterilised jar.
Simmer the vinegar and seasoning. Pour over the vegetables and allow to cool. 10–15 minutes.

SICHUAN-STYLE PICKLES

There's something really rewarding about fermented pickles made the traditional way. The combination of salt, water and time allows the complexities of natural fermentation (in this case lacto-fermentation) to take place and create unique flavours. Sichuan-style pickles are made using added spices and chilli to really lift the aroma. They are commonly eaten as a side dish or palate refresher.

MAKES 2 LITRE (70 FL OZ) JAR; SUGGESTED SERVING SIZE 50 G (1¾ OZ) PER PERSON

Pickling liquid
- ½ cup salt
- 1 litre (35 fl oz) water
- 2 tablespoons Sichuan peppercorns
- 3 star anise
- 20 g (¾ oz) fresh ginger, sliced
- ½ cup vodka or baijiu (Chinese spirit, 40–60 per cent proof)

- 100 g (3½ oz) green beans, washed well, stems trimmed and cut in half
- ¼ cabbage (150 g/5½ oz), washed well and cut into large chunks
- 200 g (7 oz) daikon, washed well, peeled and cut into batons 5 cm x 1 cm (2 in x ½ in)
- 1 carrot (200 g/7 oz), washed well, peeled and cut into 5 mm (¼ in) thick discs
- 5 long red chillis, washed well, deseeded if desired and cut into 3 cm (1¼ in) pieces

For the picking liquid, bring the salt and water to a simmer in a pot. Once at a simmer, remove from the heat and allow to cool to room temperature.

Pour this liquid into a sterilised, dry 2 litre (70 fl oz) jar and add the Sichuan peppercorns, star anise, ginger and alcohol.

In a small pot of boiling water, blanch the green beans for 5-10 seconds then drain. This will remove the raw green flavour from them.

Add the green beans and the rest of the vegetables to the jar, ensuring they are submerged in the pickling liquid. Store for at least 1 week in a dark space before eating. Always use a clean utensil when handling to prevent spoilage.

You can reuse the pickling liquid when the vegetables have been consumed by topping it up with more water boiled with salt and more spices as required, adding 1-2 tablespoons of alcohol with each batch.

THE LOWDOWN

Heat the water and salt together, allow to cool. Pour the liquids and spices into a sterilised jar. Clean and cut the veges, blanch the beans and submerge in the liquid. 1 hour for prep with minimum 7 days of pickle time.

BEANCURD-FERMENTED CHINESE CABBAGE

This is a recipe I created a while ago inspired by Korean kimchi, more specifically the white kimchi variety where the cabbage requires minimal fermenting time so it's clean in flavour, bright and refreshing.

This is a great staple to have in the fridge to serve on its own in the middle of the table, or chopped and used in a stir-fry or fried rice. I also love it chopped and stirred through mayonnaise as a sauce or dip or in a sandwich.

It's incredibly easy to make and gets better with age. It's delicious after a week and if properly stored in the fridge will keep for a couple of months.

MAKES 1 LITRE (35 FL OZ) JAR; SUGGESTED SERVING SIZE 30 G (1 OZ) PER PERSON

- 1 medium wombok (napa/Chinese cabbage) approx. 800 g–1.2 kg (1 lb 12 oz–2 lb 10 oz)
- 2 tablespoons salt
- 200 g (7 oz) fermented beancurd (curds and liquid)
- ½ cup rice vinegar (white vinegar or apple cider vinegar also work well)
- 20 g (¾ oz) fresh ginger, roughly chopped
- 5 cloves garlic
- 3 tablespoons sugar
- 2 small red chillis, finely chopped (optional)

Wash the wombok well and remove the core. Cut the wombok into 3 cm (1¼ in) segments, separate and place in a large bowl. Sprinkle and mix the salt through the wombok to start drawing out the moisture and begin the wilting process. Leave for at least 1 hour or overnight. Drain off any liquid that has been drawn out of the cabbage.

In a food processor or blender, blitz the rest of the ingredients, except the chilli, until well blended. Pour the mixture over the cabbage and mix through with the chillis, if using. Store the marinated cabbage in a sterilised, dry 1 litre (35 fl oz) jar or airtight container in the fridge.

THE LOWDOWN

Salt the cut wombok, let sit for 1 hour or overnight, then drain. Blitz the remaining ingredients and mix through the cabbage. Leave to ferment for at least 1 day and up to 2 months in a jar or container in the fridge. Approx. 15 minutes of prep, overnight salting and at least 1 day fermenting.

SMASHED CUCUMBER SALAD

Every region in China will tend to have their own version of this dish; however, the one I constantly crave is the garlicky spicy kind. The simple mix of soy sauce, chilli oil and raw garlic is such a classic central Chinese flavour that has grown to be very popular in the West too.

This salad is a perfect palate refresher for the table and is packed with flavour, with salivating qualities to make you go back for more until it's all gone. It's so easy to make and a guaranteed people-pleaser.

The great thing about this recipe is that you can substitute so many other vegetables for the cucumbers, such as blanched green beans, steamed broccoli or cooked broad beans. The real hero of this dish is the seasoning combination.

Feel free to garnish with chopped spring onion, coriander or fried peanuts for that little something extra.

Cut the cucumber in half lengthways and use a spoon to remove the seeds. Lay each cucumber half cut-side down on a cutting board and use the side of a cleaver or large knife, or a rolling pin, to smash it until it splits open. The smashing creates crevices for the sauce to seep into and carry the seasoning. Don't go overboard though: you don't want to obliterate it!

Place the cucumber in a bowl with the salt and leave for at least 10 minutes. Drain any liquid that has been drawn out during the salting process.

Add the rest of the ingredients to the cucumber and toss everything together.

SERVES 2-4 AS A COLD SIDE WITH RICE

1 large telegraph cucumber (300–500 g/10½ oz–1 lb 2 oz), washed
1½ teaspoons salt
5 cloves garlic, minced
2 teaspoons black vinegar
1 tablespoon white vinegar
pinch of white pepper
1½ tablespoons light soy sauce
2 teaspoons sugar
1 teaspoon sesame oil (optional)
2–3 tablespoons chilli oil (depending on spice level)

THE LOWDOWN

Clean and cut the cucumber. Smash then salt to draw out the liquid. Season. Approx. 15 minutes.

Apps, Bites & Snacks

WOOD EAR FUNGUS SALAD

Wood ear or black cloud ear mushroom is a fungus that grows in the shape of a wrinkled ear on damp wood. You can buy them fresh, but you'll most likely find them dehydrated in the dry goods aisle at your local Asian supermarket. They are super light and easily rehydrated for consumption.

This is an easy side dish that makes a great accompaniment for banquets as it has an interesting 'electric' crisp texture, making for a lovely textural difference between bites of different dishes at the table.

If buying fresh, try buying smaller, young wood ear fungus as they tend to be more tender, which is what you want for this preparation; the larger, older ones are better for stews and casseroles.

If using dried wood ear fungus, in a bowl rehydrate in 1 litre (35 fl oz) of hot water from the kettle for at least 30 minutes, until tender. Drain and pat dry with a clean tea towel, as any excess moisture will dilute the seasoning.

Cut or rip larger wood ear fungus into 3-4 cm (1¼-1½ in) pieces.

In a bowl, mix the fungus with the other ingredients, adjusting the seasoning if needed.

SERVES 2-4 AS A COLD SIDE WITH RICE

150 g (5½ oz) fresh or 20-25 g (¾-1 oz) dried wood ear fungus
2 cloves garlic, minced
1 tablespoon rice vinegar or white vinegar
1 teaspoon sugar
½ teaspoon salt
1 tablespoon light soy sauce
1 teaspoon sesame oil
1 small chilli, chopped (optional)
small handful of fresh coriander, chopped

THE LOWDOWN

Rehydrate dried wood ear fungus, dry well and season. 35 minutes.

JUICY PRAWN TOAST

What's not to love about prawn toast? This crunchy, juicy and incredibly easy yum cha classic is flavourful enough to wow any foodie. The main ingredients are leftover bread and frozen prawns so it makes an excellent snack (ready in under 15 minutes!), or rustle some up when guests pop over and you want to impress.

If using frozen prawns, thaw in a medium-sized bowl of cold water, soaking the prawns until soft. When thawed, pour out the water and remove the shells (if using whole prawns). Pat dry with a paper towel.

Devein the prawns by cutting a small slit across the back to expose the vein and pulling it out to discard. Use a cleaver or a chef's knife to chop the prawns into a paste (I like to keep it a little chunky for texture). Alternatively, put the prawn meat into a small food processor or chopper and blitz into a paste (but not too smooth).

Season with the sesame oil, salt, sugar and white pepper, then, using chopsticks or your clean fingers, mix in the egg white in a circular motion for about 2 minutes. The paste will thicken as you mix.

Evenly spread 2-3 tablespoons of prawn paste on each bread slice and sprinkle over the sesame seeds to cover the top. Lightly pat the sesame seeds down so they stick, and shake off the excess.

In a large pan, heat the oil to 170°C (325°F), or until the oil bubbles around a wooden chopstick when you dip it in. Shallow-fry the prawn toast over a medium heat for about 3 minutes on each side.

Cut each slice on the diagonal and serve with mayonnaise.

MAKES 12 PIECES

300 g (10½ oz) raw prawn meat (fresh or frozen)
2 teaspoons sesame oil
½ teaspoon salt
1 teaspoon sugar
pinch of white pepper
1 egg white
6 thick slices of bread, crust removed if desired (use soft white loaf or sourdough)
3 tablespoons sesame seeds
200 ml (7 fl oz) cooking oil for frying
Japanese-style mayonnaise to serve (optional)

THE LOWDOWN

Clean and chop or blitz the prawns into a paste and mix with the seasoning. Spread on sliced bread, top with sesame seeds and shallow-fry in oil for about 3 minutes on each side.
15–20 minutes.

PORK BELLY GUA BAO

In the early 2000s, influential Asian-American celebrity chefs David Chang and Eddie Huang popularised the classic Taiwanese street snack gua bao — flat steamed buns that fold out to be filled with meat, veges and condiments. It hasn't taken long for these filled buns to make their way onto the menu in cocktail bars and cafés across Australia and New Zealand.

Gua bao are often found in the frozen section of large supermarkets and most Asian grocers. They're a great staple for your freezer as they come in handy when struggling to think of what to serve unexpected guests. I love to serve them with this fatty pork belly that's been braised in a rich, savoury soy broth until it's soft and unctuous.

MAKES 12 GUA BAO

Braised pork belly
- 800 g–1 kg (1 lb 12 oz–2 lb 4 oz) pork belly (choose a piece that has some decent fat on it, minimum 20 per cent)
- 600 ml (21 fl oz) water
- ⅓ cup light soy sauce
- ½ cup sugar
- 3 tablespoons salt
- ½ teaspoon white pepper
- 1 small brown onion, roughly chopped
- 6 cloves garlic, roughly chopped
- 30 g (1 oz) fresh ginger, sliced
- 3 star anise
- 6 cloves

To serve
- 12 pack frozen gua bao
- hot mustard to taste
- 1 telegraph cucumber, cut into 3 mm-thick (⅛ in) slices

Cut the pork belly into 15 cm x 7 cm (6 in x 2¾ in) chunks. Place the pork and all the remaining ingredients in a medium-sized pot and bring to a gentle simmer. Turn the heat down to low, cover the pot and braise for 45-60 minutes until you can poke through the meat with a knife or chopstick without much resistance. At this point take out the pork and chill in the fridge overnight or until it's cool enough to slice. Strain the braising liquid and reserve.

When ready to assemble and serve your bao, simmer the braising liquid in a small pot over a medium heat until it has reduced by half and thickened slightly.

Cut the cold pork belly into slices to fit your bao — 2 cm (¾ in) thickness works well — and pan-fry for 3 minutes on each side. You could also bake in an oven preheated to 200°C (400°F) for 10 minutes until hot. Pour the hot reduced braising liquid over the heated pork.

Follow the reheating instructions for your store-bought gua bao, usually they're steamed over a pot of water in a basket or microwaved until hot.

Open up the bao, brush the inside with mustard to taste, place a slice of the pork belly coated in the sauce inside the bao, top with a slice of cucumber, close the bao and you're done. Serve hot.

THE LOWDOWN

In a pot braise the pork, seasoning and water until soft. Chill the pork and slice. Reduce and thicken sauce. Reheat pork slices and sauce to fill the heated-up store-bought gua bao. Approx. 1 hour for pork and allow for cooling, ideally done the day before serving.

CLASSIC DUMPLINGS

The word dumplings in Chinese is a blanket term for many types of food, from sweets like glutinous rice flour balls, to steamed savoury rice packages filled with pork and salted egg yolk. More often than not it refers to food in parcels or wrapped in a sort of pastry.

These northern-style dumplings are perhaps the best known and are very much seen as a Chinese classic in the Western world. They are the perfect little package in every bite, carby and comforting and filled with well-seasoned protein and vegetables for texture.

I've grown up on these and they are the perfect food to store in the freezer for those days when you don't know what to make. Just pop them in a pot of boiling water or in a fry pan to cook from frozen. They also make a great hosting activity: welcome a small crowd of guests around the kitchen bench and get everyone involved in the making process — it's fun, interactive and, the best part, everyone helps out with the wrapping.

The following are examples of the types of filling variations you can use, how to prepare homemade wrappers (aka skins), and different cooking techniques. Most of the time I buy pre-rolled fresh wrappers from Asian grocers as it's convenient and affordable. Every time I make dumplings I make about a hundred at a time so that I can freeze the leftovers as a gift to my future self.

PORK AND PRAWN DUMPLING FILLING

The combination of fatty pork mince and prawn bits is an absolute classic Cantonese protein pairing. The flavours are a great 'surf and turf' combination and also a beautifully textural experience. To really amp up the aroma, sometimes I like to fry the aromatics (spring onion, garlic and ginger) for a minute in a bit of oil before mixing into the proteins.

Asian grocers tend to have lean and fatty pork mince options available if they have a butchery section.

In a large bowl, mix all the ingredients together vigorously for 5 minutes. The constant working and mixing of the pork mince will activate the meat fibres and allow the mince to combine better, creating a denser texture when cooked.

Before committing to the filling, microwave a teaspoon of the mix for 45 seconds, or until cooked, then taste and adjust the seasoning if needed.

MAKES ENOUGH TO FILL 80-100 DUMPLINGS

700 g (1 lb 9 oz) fatty pork mince (20-30 per cent fat)
300 g (10½ oz) raw prawns (frozen or fresh), shelled, cleaned and roughly chopped
3 cloves garlic, minced
30 g (1 oz) fresh ginger, minced
2 spring onions, finely chopped
1 egg
¼ teaspoon white pepper
1½ tablespoons cornflour
2 teaspoons chicken bouillon powder (optional)
1 tablespoon salt
1 tablespoon light soy sauce
2 tablespoons sugar
3 tablespoons rice wine

THE LOWDOWN

In a bowl, mix all the ingredients together, test-cook a sample, adjust the seasoning if necessary, and it's ready to wrap! Approx. 20 mins.

CHICKEN AND SWEETCORN DUMPLING FILLING

Chicken and sweetcorn is a fairly common pairing as they work so well together. The way chicken can carry most types of seasoning means you can add ingredients that are subtle in flavour. The corn adds a pop of sweetness and a textural complexity to the filling. If you have access to fresh corn, even better!

In a large bowl, mix all the ingredients together vigorously for 5 minutes. The constant working and mixing of the chicken mince will allow the water to bind with the protein more effectively and will result in a juicier filling, especially given the lack of fat in the mix.

Before committing to the filling, microwave a teaspoon of the mix for 45 seconds, or until cooked, then taste and adjust the seasoning if needed.

MAKES ENOUGH TO FILL 80–100 DUMPLINGS

800 g (1 lb 12 oz) chicken mince
400 g (14 oz) can whole corn kernels, drained, or 1½ cups frozen corn kernels, thawed
3 cloves garlic, minced
30 g (1 oz) fresh ginger, minced
2 spring onions, finely chopped
1 egg
¼ teaspoon white pepper
1½ tablespoons cornflour
2 teaspoons chicken bouillon powder (optional)
1 tablespoon salt
2 tablespoons sugar
2 tablespoons rice wine
½ cup water

THE LOWDOWN

In a bowl, mix all the ingredients together, test-cook a sample, adjust the seasoning if necessary, and it's ready to wrap! Approx. 15 minutes.

TOFU AND MUSHROOM DUMPLING FILLING

I'm often asked for vegetarian/vegan dumpling filling ideas, but many of the options compromise flavour and protein content. Here I have created my favourite (to date!) vegan dumpling filling that is incredibly delicious — like, incredibly so! This will honestly beat any other versions of this filling out there . . . in my humble opinion.

Break the tofu into a food processor, add the rehydrated mushrooms and blitz for 10 seconds or until finely chopped.

Preheat a large pan or wok, add the oil and fry the garlic, ginger and spring onion over a high heat for 1 minute until aromatic. Add the mushroom and tofu blend, and cook for 5 minutes to remove some of the excess moisture. Add the remaining ingredients, except the slurry and sesame oil, and cook for a further 5 minutes. Taste and adjust the seasoning if necessary.

Stir in the slurry and turn off the heat, then pour in the sesame oil and stir through. Place in a container and allow to cool completely, ideally overnight in the fridge, before using.

MAKES ENOUGH TO FILL 80-100 DUMPLINGS

- 1 cup or 10 medium-sized dried shiitake mushrooms, soaked in warm water for 2 hours or overnight, then drained and squeezed
- ½ cup or 20 g (¾ oz) dried wood ear fungus, soaked in warm water for 2 hours or overnight, then drained and squeezed
- ¼ cup oil
- 3 cloves garlic, minced
- 30 g (1 oz) fresh ginger, minced
- 3 spring onions, finely chopped
- 150 g (5½ oz) spinach leaves
- ¼ teaspoon white pepper
- 1 tablespoon salt
- 2 tablespoons light soy sauce
- 2 tablespoons sugar
- 2 tablespoons preserved olive vegetable (optional)
- 1½ tablespoons cornflour mixed with 1 tablespoon water to make a thickening slurry
- 1 tablespoon sesame oil

THE LOWDOWN

In a food processor, blitz the tofu and soaked mushrooms and fry in a pan with the oil and aromatics. Add the remaining ingredients, except the slurry and sesame oil, and cook. Thicken with slurry, stir through the sesame oil and chill overnight before wrapping. Approx. 20 minutes with rehydration of mushrooms 2 hours.

BASIC DUMPLING WRAPPERS

Making your own dumpling wrappers is extremely rewarding, and homemade tends to have a more of a QQ bounce to them. (QQ is the equivalent to al dente in a Chinese context). The best part is that they're so easy to make! However, there is no shame to store-bought — nine times out of ten I buy store bought.

MAKES 50-60 WRAPPERS

400 g (14 oz) plain flour
240 ml (8 fl oz) warm water (hot water from the tap is perfect)
Extra flour for dusting

Start with the flour in a medium-sized bowl and slowly pour the warm water into the centre of the flour, stirring with chopsticks or a wooden spoon. Mix until there is no visible dry flour left in the bowl; at this stage it should look like a bowl of small bits of dough. Go in with your clean hands now and knead the dough for 3-4 minutes until well combined into a ball (if it feels too sticky, add more flour). Cover the bowl with cling film or a damp tea towel and let it rest for at least 30 minutes.

The dough now should look smooth. If not rest it a little longer.

Place the dough on a clean surface and cut it into four even sections. Take each section and roll it out by hand into a log shape about 2 cm (¾ in) thick. While working with the dough, any sections that aren't in use should sit under a damp tea towel on the bench to prevent them from drying out.

Section one of your four logs into thumb-tip-sized cuts (about 2 cm [¾ in]). Each piece should weigh about 9-11 g (¼ oz). Take a piece and on a floured surface press the dough down with your palms to pre-flatten into a disc, then use a light rolling pin or wooden stick (even a plastic cup works well) to roll it out flat until the disc is 2 mm (1/16 in) thickness and about 7-8 cm (2¾-3¼ in) in diameter. Optional but ideal: try to roll the edge of the disc thinner than the centre by rotating the disc from the centre with one hand and with the other, roll the dough away from you starting from the middle.

Repeat with the remaining sections. You may stack the rolled discs, making sure to flour each one before stacking, then cover with the damp tea towel.

The wrappers can be stored in the freezer in airtight bags.

THE LOWDOWN

In a bowl, mix the flour and warm water, then rest the dough. Cut the dough into four pieces and roll them into logs. Cut them into thumb-tip-sized pieces, then flatten each piece and roll into a thin disc. Stack the discs with flour in between. Approx. 40 minutes (includes 30 minutes for dough resting).

Wrapping the dumplings

Spoon about 1 tablespoon of filling into the middle of each store-bought or homemade wrapper. Dip your fingers into a small container of water and wet the edge of the skin — two smears will do. Bring the opposite ends of the wrapper together and seal by pleating from one edge to the other or just close them together and apply pressure to seal the sides.

There's no rule for wrapping dumplings. The main objective is to enclose the parcel so the filling doesn't seep out when being cooked. The best way to learn wrapping is to watch videos online or get an experienced friend to show you.

Boiled dumplings

Boiled dumplings are super quick and easy to prepare and make great carriers of sauces and seasoning oils. I often serve them alongside black vinegar, light soy sauce and chilli oil mixed together as a dip. Try equal parts to start, and adjust to your liking.

Choose a medium or large pot depending on the size of your batch. Fill with water and bring to a boil.

For fresh:
Drop in the dumplings and bring it back to a boil, then reduce the heat to low and cook the dumplings until they float to the surface and stay there for 1 minute. Total cook time is about 6–8 minutes.

Using a slotted spoon or spider, scoop them out and place in a bowl. To prevent them from sticking, drizzle 2 teaspoons of oil over the dumplings and mix gently, if desired.

For frozen:
Drop in the dumplings and bring it back to a boil, then pour in a cup of cold water, which will slow down the cooking process so the wrappers won't overcook before the heat can get to the filling. Bring the pot back to a boil, reduce the heat to low and cook until they float to the surface for 3 minutes. Total cook time is about 14–16 minutes. Using a slotted spoon or spider, scoop them out and place in a bowl. To prevent them from sticking, drizzle 2 teaspoons of oil over the dumplings and mix gently, if desired.

Pan-fried dumplings

Start by boiling the dumplings until cooked through using the method above. Heat up a non-stick fry pan and fry the dumplings flat-side down on medium heat until golden brown.

DUMPLINGS PAN-FRIED WITH A CRISPY BASE

This is my favourite way of cooking dumplings, flavourful with crazy-good textures going on. The crispy savoury base, also known as a 'dumpling skirt', is essentially a thin pancake batter that's poured over the fresh or frozen dumplings and cooked until the liquid has evaporated and the batter is crisped up on the base.

Mix the batter ingredients in a bowl or jug. You'll use all of this batter to 'skirt' a large batch of about 30 dumplings, and about two-thirds for a medium batch.

Choose an appropriate size non-stick fry pan with a lid, to suit the size of your batch. There should be at least a 1 cm (½ in) gap between dumplings.

Heat the oil over a medium heat and arrange the dumplings flat-side down. Fry for a few minutes, or until the dumplings are slightly golden on the base.

Pour the right amount of batter over the dumplings and reduce the heat to medium-low. Cover and steam for 8 minutes for fresh dumplings and 14 minutes for frozen (no thawing required). When the skins start to look translucent, remove the lid and cook the batter until all liquid has evaporated and a crispy base is formed. Turn off the heat.

Use a non-scratch spatula to carefully loosen the edges of the batter and move the base around. If the whole skirt is sliding in the pan, it is ready to flip onto a serving plate. Place a plate over the dumpling pan, hold it in place, flip the pan over, and release! The dumplings should be on the serving plate with the skirt on top.

Batter mix

200 ml (7 fl oz) water
1 tablespoon oil
1 tablespoon cornflour
1½ tablespoons plain flour
1 teaspoon chicken bouillon powder or ½ teaspoon salt

To cook

1 tablespoon oil

THE LOWDOWN

Fry the dumplings, add the batter and cover. When cooked, remove the lid and allow the base to get crispy. Flip onto a serving plate. 20–25 minutes.

Patience

This is how time moved in Por Por's kitchen:
slow like dough rising in the sun, fast like the stories
told around the mahjong table. Time was hidden in
the folds of every dumpling and sealed in every bao.
Roast duck, soups and congee were all-day affairs —
we watched steaming pots and quivering lids as if
they might reveal our fortunes. Time is also what gave
the wok its supersonic flash, the melodic clash of
steel upon steel that got louder as dinner got closer.
Giving us kids a job would keep us still. It's here,
our oversized aprons dusted in rice flour and fingers
slicked with grease, that we learned the meaning
of patience — when to pause for breath, when to let
time work its magic. Ceramic jars filled with homemade
pickles, salted eggs and pungent rice wine lurked at
the back of the pantry. Everything worth waiting for
revealed itself after hours, sometimes days, or weeks.

Chris Tse
New Zealand Poet Laureate, 2022–2024

SOUPS & BROTHS

BASIC PORK BROTH

Broths are often overlooked when curating a banquet for guests. Most Cantonese restaurants serve them to accompany the meal, and I believe they are one of the most important elements in a well-thought-out and balanced dining experience.

Broths are light and versatile, used mainly to whet the appetite before the meal starts and to act as a palate cleanser, with sips taken after eating foods that are intensely seasoned so the next bite will be as exciting as the first.

Following are a few recipes for basic broths. If you remove the carrot and add-ons, they are essentially basic stocks that can be used in other recipes to replace water, adding more complexity. They freeze well for up to three months.

This first step is optional but will help give you a cleaner, clearer broth. Submerge the pork in water in a large pot and bring to a boil. Turn off the heat, then pour the water out and rinse the meat under cold running water for about 30 seconds. Alternatively, rinse the pork shoulder in the sink in a large bowl with hot tap water or a kettle of boiling water, then rinse with cold water for 30 seconds. This is to remove impurities and blood from the meat.

In a large pot, put the rinsed meat, and all the other ingredients. Bring to a boil, then reduce the heat to a gentle simmer. Allow to simmer for anywhere between 1 and 2 hours, skimming any impurities from the surface of the broth every now and then. Taste and adjust the seasoning if necessary. Remove from the heat when it reaches your desired taste.

Serve a small bowl of the broth to each guest or place in the middle of the table in a large vessel with a ladle so they can help themselves.

If the pork shoulder isn't completely broken down, I love to serve it on a plate with a drizzle of soy sauce and chilli oil over the top as an extra dish.

SERVES 10-12

600–800 g (1 lb 5 oz–1 lb 12 oz) pork shoulder (with skin and fat, bone-in optional)
3–4 litres (105–140 fl oz) water
20 g (¾ oz) fresh ginger, sliced
3 cloves garlic, smacked
2 spring onions, cut into thirds
¼ teaspoon white pepper
1 tablespoon salt or to taste
2 carrots, cut into 4 cm (1½ in) chunks

Optional add-ons

5 dried shiitake mushrooms
80 g (2¾ oz) dehydrated bok choy (found at your local Asian grocer)
2 tablespoons dried goji berries
5 dried dates

THE LOWDOWN

Boil or rinse the pork with hot water. Simmer the pork in water, aromatics and your desired veges for 1–2 hours. Serve the pork with seasoning as an extra dish!

Chicken variation

Using the same recipe, replace the pork with chicken carcasses and/or chicken thighs and wings — about 600–800 g (1 lb 5 oz–1 lb 12 oz) will do the trick. Rinse with hot water for the initial step to remove impurities for a clearer broth. The simmer time of this would be less than the pork version — 1 hour would be plenty.

THE LOWDOWN

Rinse the chicken with hot water. Simmer the chicken with water, aromatics and your desired veges for 1 hour.

Vegetarian variation

Using the same recipe, remove the meat component and try to use as many of the optional add-ons as possible to add complexity to the broth. I would double all the dried ingredients to amp up the flavour and simmer for about 1 hour.

THE LOWDOWN

Simmer the dried and fresh veges with water and aromatics for 1 hour.

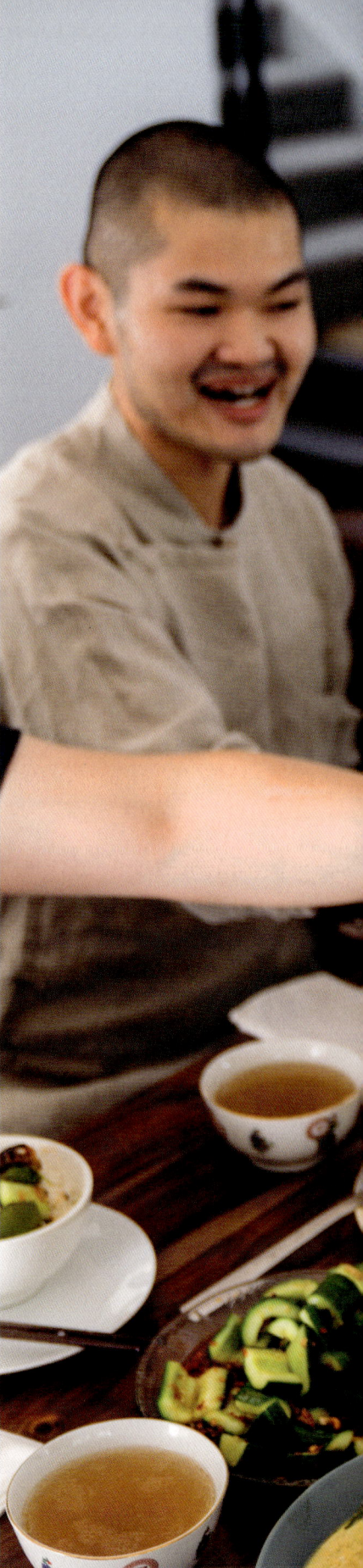

SUPREME CHICKEN MASTER BROTH

This broth is really complex with rich umami flavours: the caramelisation of the roasted chicken and sweet, savoury, seafood flavours of the dried scallops are what makes it so special. I love serving boiled wontons in this broth or add your favourite noodles to make an incredible chicken and noodle soup.

Preheat the oven to 220°C (425°F).

In a large bowl, mix the oil, chicken, salt, white pepper, ginger, garlic and spring onion together and lay evenly in a large baking dish. Roast the chicken for about 30 minutes until golden brown, shaking and flipping the pieces of chicken about 20 minutes into the roast for even browning.

Place the water in a large pot and set it over a high heat. Add in the roasted chicken, including any cooking juices, and all the rest of the ingredients. Bring to a gentle boil, then turn down the heat to a low gentle simmer. Simmer for 60-80 minutes or until it tastes rich and complex, skimming any impurities from the surface of the broth every now and then. Taste and adjust the seasoning if necessary.

If storing for future use, pour the broth into containers to freeze.

SERVES 10-12

3 tablespoons oil
800 g (1 lb 12 oz) chicken carcasses (chicken frames)
500 g (1 lb 2 oz) chicken wings
1½ tablespoons salt or to taste
¼ teaspoon white pepper
30 g (1 oz) fresh ginger, sliced
6 cloves garlic, smacked
4 spring onions, cut into thirds
3–4 litres (105–140 fl oz) water
5 dried shiitake mushrooms
40 g (1½ oz) dried scallops or dried prawns

Optional add-ons
3 tablespoons dried goji berries
6 dried dates

THE LOWDOWN

Roast the chicken and aromatics in the oven. Simmer the roasted chicken in water and other ingredients for 60–80 minutes.

QUICK AND EASY SWEETCORN SOUP

As a child I spent the majority of my spare time at my parents' Chinese takeaway shop, and this soup was a classic on all the menu boards. It is perhaps the gateway soup for many into a particular type of Chinese soup named 'egg drop', where a soup is thickened with cornflour and whisked egg. It's a dish that is very much created by assimilating whatever ingredients are available to us — extremely simple to make and comforting for the soul.

Here and over the page are a couple of versions of this classic, the simplest version using canned corn, just like takeaways, and my modern take on creamy chicken sweetcorn soup, utilising fresh corn when in season.

Place all the ingredients, except the spring onion greens, chicken, slurry and egg in a medium-sized pot and gently simmer for 10 minutes.

Add the chicken, if using, and stir for 2 minutes. Slowly stir in as much of the slurry as needed to reach your desired consistency — it should resemble a thick pouring gravy. Gently stir through the whisked egg then turn off the heat. Serve garnished with the spring onion greens.

SERVES 10–12

- 400 g (14 oz) can creamed corn
- 2 cups or 250 g (9 oz) frozen mixed vegetables (carrot, peas and corn) or frozen corn kernels
- 3 cloves garlic, minced
- 20 g (¾ oz) fresh ginger, minced
- 1.5 litres (52 fl oz) water or stock
- 1 tablespoon salt
- white pepper, to taste
- 2 teaspoons sugar
- 2 spring onions, greens and whites sliced separately
- 300 g (10½ oz) skinless boneless chicken thigh or breast, cubed 1 cm (½ in) (optional)
- ¼ cup cornflour mixed with ¼ cup water to make a thickening slurry
- 1 egg, whisked in a small bowl

THE LOWDOWN

Add the ingredients to a pot and bring to a simmer. Thicken soup with slurry and egg. Approx. 20 minutes.

BANQUET-STYLE CHICKEN AND SWEETCORN SOUP

There's nothing like fresh corn off the cob in season, and this soup is just so warming and comforting. The mushrooms add a degree of savouriness and texture.

SERVES 10–12

Chicken
2 boneless skinless chicken thigh or breast (1 cm [½ in] cubes)
½ teaspoon baking soda
pinch of white pepper
2 teaspoons cornflower
2 teaspoons salt
50 ml (1½ fl oz) water

5 fresh corn cobs or 500 g (1 lb 2 oz) canned or frozen whole corn kernels
3 cloves garlic, minced
20 g (¾ oz) fresh ginger, minced
2 litres (70 fl oz) water or stock
1 tablespoon salt
white pepper to taste
2 teaspoons sugar
2 spring onions
100 g (3½ oz) fresh enoki mushrooms, cut into 3 pieces about 4 cm (1½ in) long
100 g (3½ oz) rehydrated shiitake mushrooms, thinly sliced (about 4 medium dried shiitake)
¼ cup cornflour mixed with ¼ cup water
1 egg, whisked in a small bowl

For the chicken, place all the ingredients in a bowl and mix very well until the water is absorbed into the chicken. This process is called 'velveting' (see page 23).

If using fresh corn cobs, remove the husk and silk (wearing rubber gloves makes this process so much easier). On a chopping board, use a knife to slice off all the kernels.

In a medium-sized pot, bring all the ingredients, except the chicken, mushrooms, slurry, egg and green spring onions, to a gentle boil for 15 minutes, stirring every now and then to prevent it burning on the bottom.

Using a slotted spoon or spider, scoop one-third of the corn kernels out and set aside. Using a stick blender, blitz the rest of the corn and the liquid until smooth (about 3 minutes). Strain the blended broth through a sieve, put it back in the pot and bring to a gentle simmer.

Return the reserved corn kernels to the pot, then add the chicken and stir for 2 minutes. Add the mushrooms. Slowly stir in as much of the slurry as needed to reach your desired consistency, it should resemble a thick pouring gravy. Gently stir through the whisked egg then turn off the heat. Serve garnished with the green spring onions.

THE LOWDOWN
Slice the kernels from fresh corn and boil gently with water and seasoning. Blitz most of it and strain back into the pot. Add the veges, whole kernels and marinated chicken. Thicken soup with slurry and egg. Approx. 35 minutes.

EASY HOT AND SOUR SOUP

This soup uses the classic egg drop gravy method where it is thickened using cornflour and egg to make it more substantial, and is a great accompaniment to any meal with rice on the side.

The unique savoury and sour flavour makes this soup particularly interesting and enticing. The acidity from the different vinegars means you're salivating as you eat it, which draws you back for spoon after spoon. This is a very simple base recipe for this kind of soup. You can add whatever ingredients you wish, such as different vegetables or your favourite protein. Any additions just need to be cut into small pieces.

SERVES 10-12

Soup

- 5 dried shiitake mushrooms, rehydrated for 20 minutes or overnight in 200 ml (7 fl oz) warm water
- 20 g (¾ oz) dried wood ear fungus, rehydrated in warm water until soft (at least 30 minutes)
- 2 tablespoons oil
- 3 cloves garlic, thinly sliced
- 20 g (¾ oz) fresh ginger, sliced into thin matchsticks
- 1 spring onion, thinly sliced
- 1 litre (35 fl oz) water or stock
- 200 g (7 oz) firm tofu, drained, patted dry and cut into 1 cm (½ in) cubes
- 100 g (3½ oz) canned bamboo shoots, drained (optional)
- 2-4 fresh chillis, chopped (optional)
- ⅓ cup cornflour mixed with ¼ cup water to make a thickening slurry

Ingredients continued on opposite page

Drain the rehydrated shiitake mushrooms, reserving the soaking liquid. Thinly slice and set aside. Drain the rehydrated wood ear fungus, discarding the soaking liquid. Slice into strips and set aside.

If using pork, place all the ingredients in a bowl and mix together until well combined. Set aside.

In a medium-sized pot over a medium heat, add the oil and fry the garlic, ginger and spring onion until aromatic, approx. 30 seconds. Add the sliced shiitake and fry for a further 2 minutes.

Add the water (or stock), reserved shiitake liquid, tofu, bamboo shoots and wood ear fungus, and bring to a simmer. Add in the pork, if using, gently stirring to separate the strips. Simmer over a low heat for 10 minutes.

Slowly stir in as much of the slurry as needed to reach your desired consistency — the soup should resemble a thick pouring gravy. You can make and add more slurry if needed.

Add the seasoning and chillis, if using. Gently stir through the whisked egg, then turn off the heat. Taste and adjust the seasoning if need be — it should be salty, savoury and sour.

Serve garnished with the coriander.

2 eggs, whisked in a small bowl
chopped fresh coriander to garnish

Seasoning
¼ cup black vinegar
¼ cup white vinegar
1½ tablespoons salt or to taste
¼ cup light soy sauce
½ teaspoon white pepper
2 tablespoons sugar
1 tablespoon sesame oil

Pork (optional)
150 g (5½ oz) lean pork, sliced into thin strips
1 tablespoon cornflour
1 teaspoon salt

THE LOWDOWN

Soak the dried mushrooms. Season the meat. Fry the aromatics in a pot. Add the vegetables and meat into the pot with the water. Season and simmer, thicken with slurry and egg. Approx. 35 minutes.

VEGES, TOFU & EGGS

QUICK STIR-FRIED CABBAGE

I feel like cabbage has always been the underdog in the vegetable world because of how common it is. But it is naturally super sweet, texturally interesting, and when slightly charred through stir-frying it has this beautiful caramelised flavour that's very addictive. Plus it's usually incredibly affordable when in season. Here's one of my favourite ways to prepare cabbage, and one of the easier dishes in this book.

SERVES 3–4

¼ cabbage (roughly 400 g/ 14 oz)
2 tablespoons oil
2 cloves garlic, minced
10 g (¼ oz) fresh ginger, sliced
pinch of white pepper
salt to taste

Prepare the cabbage by cutting it into 3 cm (1¼ in) cubes. Start by removing the core then cut 3 cm (1¼ in) thick strips lengthways, then turn it 90 degrees and cut it the same as before. This should give you even-sized pieces. Squeeze and pull apart any sections that are stuck together, and set aside.

In a heated pan or wok over a high heat, add the oil and evenly spread the cabbage to start cooking, allowing it to slightly char. Try to not move the cabbage for 2 minutes to allow for caramelisation to occur and for some parts to char.

Add in the garlic, ginger and seasoning and stir-fry for a few more minutes, or until the cabbage is cooked through. It should be slightly tender but still crisp, and almost transparent on the thinner leaves.

THE LOWDOWN

Cut the cabbage and stir-fry with oil in a large pan/wok. Add aromatics and seasoning and stir-fry for a few more minutes. Approx. 10 minutes.

BOK CHOY STIR-FRY

A classic side dish for when you are trying to balance out your meals or to add that token green to a banquet, that's tasty, easy and fast! Like mere minutes fast!

Depending on the size of the bok choy, cooking time should be adjusted. I look for a slight crisp on the bok choy; however, the preferred doneness is totally up to you!

Prepare the bok choy by cutting a cross section of the base of the bok choy bulb and pulling it apart — this will divide your bok choy into sections and make it so much easier to clean. Rinse the quartered bok choy in cold water. I like to shake it vigorously in a bowl of cold water or in a filled sink to get into the muddy nooks of the segments.

In a heated large fry pan or wok, fry the ginger and garlic in the oil for 30 seconds over a high heat until they have slightly coloured golden brown. This really perfumes the oil that will coat the vegetables.

Add the bok choy, soy sauce, rice wine and seasoning, shake or toss to coat the vegetables and cover and cook for 3-4 minutes.

Remove the lid and add the slurry. Mix through for 1 minute until well combined.

SERVES 2-3

300–400 g (10½–14 oz) bok choy, quartered
30 g (1 oz) fresh ginger, thinly sliced
4 cloves garlic, roughly chopped
2 tablespoons cooking oil
2 teaspoons light soy sauce
1 tablespoon rice wine
pinch of white pepper
½ teaspoon salt
2 teaspoons sugar
1 teaspoon cornflour mixed with 2 tablespoons water to make a thickening slurry

THE LOWDOWN

Segment the bok choy and clean. Fry the aromatics in a pan with bok choy, add seasoning, thicken with slurry. Approx. 10 minutes.

BLANCHED GAI LAN WITH OYSTER SAUCE

Gai lan, or Chinese broccoli, is a nutritious vegetable from the brassica family and another classic at the Chinese banquet dinner table. It's often seen wheeled around on dim sum trolleys at yum cha as the token green — but a very tasty and craveable token green might I add. The crunchy exterior and the sweet tender middle make this one of my all-time favourite vegetables, and it's an excellent carrier of sauces.

To mix it up, bok choy, broccoli, broccolini or bean sprouts would also work perfectly with this cooking method.

Prepare your gai lan by cutting it into 6-8 cm (2½-3¼ in) lengths. If the gai lan stems are thick (over 1 cm [½ in]) diameter) cut them in half lengthways. Separate the stems and the leafy parts as they take different times to cook.

In a medium-sized pot or wok, bring the water to a gentle boil. Add all the ingredients except the gai lan and oyster sauce. Put the stems of the gai lan into the water for 2 minutes then add the leafy parts for 2 minutes, submerging them into the water. Turn off the heat.

Use a spider or tongs to take out the gai lan, shaking off the excess water.

Arrange the gai lan on a plate with the stems all facing the same direction for aesthetic purposes, just like at yum cha. Pour the oyster sauce over the top of the vegetables and serve immediately.

SERVES 2-3

400 g (14 oz) gai lan, rinsed
1 litre (35 fl oz) water
4 cloves garlic, smacked
30 g (1 oz) fresh ginger, thinly sliced
pinch of white pepper
1 tablespoon salt
1 tablespoon sugar
2 tablespoons cooking oil
3-4 tablespoons oyster sauce to serve

THE LOWDOWN

In a pot of boiling seasoned water, blanch the gai lan for 4 minutes. Serve on a plate and drizzle over oyster sauce. Approx. 10 minutes.

WATERCRESS COOKED IN BROTH

Watercress, with its fresh green grassy smell and slighty sweet taste, is rich in nostalgia for me. It could be that growing up my parents would make Chinese pork bone and watercress soup, where the broth was rich in savoury pork flavour and balanced with the sweet and fresh watercress. Perhaps it's the times I used to sell boil-up (a pork and vegetable dish, a classic in Māori cuisine) at the Avondale flea market in Auckland as a teen working in a food truck. Or maybe it's the fact that there was this uniting flavour between the two cultures that I grew to love and this made me feel comfort and familiarity.

When it comes to watercress, the degree of cooking is totally up to you. As my parents got older they would boil the life out of the watercress so it was easier to chew. This also amps up the sweetness of the broth, so they would often spoon the broth into rice and eat it together.

To mix it up or to substitute the watercress, most leafy greens would work well — just adjust cooking times for different vegetables. For me, spinach and mustard greens cooked with this method is a staple.

Cut the watercress into 6–8 cm (2½–3¼ in) lengths and pop into a bowl for rinsing. Fill the bowl with water and agitate the watercress with your fingers to remove any trapped dirt. Pour out the water.

In a medium-sized pot or wok, bring the water to a gentle boil. Add the remaining ingredients, except the century egg. Taste and adjust the seasoning if necessary — the broth should taste slightly too salty, because the watercress will dilute it and add sweetness.

Add the watercress and cook for 3–5 minutes depending on the tenderness of your watercress. Young watercress will take less time to cook whilst the larger, older watercress will take longer to break down. Taste a stem during the cook to check.

When done, turn off the heat and gently stir in the century egg. Serve in a bowl with the century egg on top of the veges.

SERVES 2–3

300 g (10½ oz) watercress
300 ml (10½ fl oz) water
1 tablespoon cooking oil
4 cloves garlic, smacked
30 g (1 oz) fresh ginger, thinly sliced
pinch of white pepper
1½ teaspoons salt
1 teaspoon sugar
2 teaspoons chicken bouillon powder
1 century egg, peeled and cut into 10 segments (optional)

THE LOWDOWN

In a pan of seasoned boiling water, blanch the watercress for a few minutes. Serve in a bowl with other ingredients and century egg (optional). Approx. 10 minutes.

SIMPLE SPICY AND TANGY STIR-FRY POTATO

It wasn't until I was in my early 20s that I had my first taste of central and northern Chinese flavours — think spicy, vinegary and aromatic with interesting spices such as Sichuan peppercorn. Having grown up in a Cantonese (southern Chinese) family, these flavours were foreign and intriguing to me.

This is one of those dishes that is super simple in concept but incredibly powerful in flavour and texture. This is a dish that's literally shredded potato cooked in a pan/wok for 2–3 minutes, but it leaves you salivating for the next time you can relive that experience.

I've given two versions here and both versions are also great served cold. It can be prepared the day before and kept in the fridge.

Julienne the potato, i.e. cut into 2-3 mm thick matchsticks (1/16-1/8 in) slices. Alternatively use a mandolin with the julienne attachment to help slice the potatoes into even thicknesses.

In a large bowl of cold water (at least 2 litres/70 fl oz), soak and agitate the cut potato for 10 minutes to remove excess starch. This will keep the potato crisp. Transfer to a colander in the sink, drain well and leave to dry.

Cut the chilli into 2 cm (¾ in) pieces. If it's too spicy for you, remove the seeds.

In a heated wok or large fry pan, add the oil and chilli and fry for 30 seconds over a medium-high heat whilst moving it around with a spatula. Do not let it blacken and burn as this will make the dish bitter.

Add the garlic, salt and white pepper and fry for another 10 seconds. Turn up the heat to high and add the dry potato juliennes. Stir-fry for 3-4 minutes until the potatoes are hot but still have a crisp crunch to them — think 'al dente' but for potatoes. Add the white vinegar to the potatoes and turn off the heat. Transfer to a plate and serve immediately.

SERVES 2-4 AS A COLD SIDE WITH RICE

- 2 medium waxy potatoes (approx 450 g/1 lb), washed and peeled if desired
- 3 medium to large dried chillis
- 2 tablespoons cooking oil
- 4 cloves garlic, sliced
- 1 teaspoon salt
- pinch of white pepper
- 2 tablespoons white vinegar

THE LOWDOWN

Cut the potato into matchsticks and soak in water. Drain well and stir-fry with oil and seasoning for a few minutes. Approx. 15–20 minutes.

THE ULTIMATE SPICY AND TANGY STIR-FRY POTATO

This version of stir-fry potato incorporates more aromatics to create a more complex and addictive flavour, using Sichuan pepper (both oil and peppercorns) and rich black vinegar. The vibrancy of the peppercorns adds a unique citrus floral aroma and, in combination with the earthy potatoes, makes this dish one of a kind.

Julienne the potato, i.e. cut into 2-3 mm (¹⁄₁₆-⅛ in) slices. Alternatively use a mandolin with the julienne attachment to help slice the potatoes into even thicknesses. Soak and drain as per previous recipe.

Deseed and slice the capsicum thinly into strips, similar sizes to the potato. Cut the chilli into 2 cm (¾ in) pieces. If it's spicy for you, remove the seeds.

In a heated wok or large fry pan, add the cooking oil, dried chilli and Sichuan peppercorns, and fry for 30 seconds over a high heat whilst moving it all around with a spatula. Do not let it blacken and burn as this will make the dish bitter.

Add the garlic, oils, salt and white pepper and fry for another 30 seconds. Add the dry potato juliennes and capsicum strips and stir-fry for 3-4 minutes until the potatoes are hot but still have a crisp crunch to them.

Add the vinegars and turn off the heat. Transfer to a plate and serve immediately.

- 2 medium waxy potatoes (approx 450 g/1 lb), washed and peeled if desired
- ½ capsicum
- 2 tablespoons cooking oil
- 3 medium to large dried chillis
- 1 teaspoon Sichuan peppercorns
- 4 cloves garlic, sliced
- ½ teaspoon Sichuan pepper oil
- 1 tablespoon chilli oil
- 1 teaspoon salt
- pinch of white pepper
- 1 tablespoon white vinegar
- 1 tablespoon black vinegar

THE LOWDOWN

Cut the potato into matchsticks and soak in water. Drain well and stir-fry with oil, capsicum strips and seasoning for a few minutes. Approx. 15–20 minutes.

SIMPLE DRY-FRY GREEN BEANS

This is one of those vegetable dishes that feels like it's in between naughty and nice; naughty because of how flavourful it is and nice because the focus is a vegetable. In Cantonese restaurants these green beans are first flash-fried (dipped into hot oil for a few seconds) and then tossed into a wok/pan to finish the cook with aromatics and seasoning. My method is much more simplified as I feel that not everyone wants to fill a pot with oil to flash-fry one dish.

Remove the top stems of the beans and cut them into 5 cm (2 in) lengths or in half.

Place the cut green beans in a heatproof bowl with the salt and 1 tablespoon of oil and mix. Pour a whole kettle of boiling water over the beans and allow to sit for 3 minutes, or until the beans are precooked — soft but with a crunch. Pour into a colander and shake the beans dry or pat dry with a paper towel. Set aside.

In a heated wok/fry pan, add the 3 tablespoons of oil and bring it up to a high heat — it needs to be hot to allow the beans to blister and create that unique texture frying gives to beans.

Add the beans and fry for 1 minute, not moving them around too much. Add the garlic, ginger, onion and chilli and stir-fry for 1 minute. Add the seasoning, preserved olive vegetable and dried preserved olives, if using. Stir-fry for another 2–3 minutes, or until everything is hot and the beans are tender. Taste and adjust the seasoning if needed.

THE LOWDOWN

Pour boiling water over the the beans to precook, drain. Wok-fry beans until blistered, and season. Approx. 15 minutes.

SERVES 2–4 AS A VEGE SIDE WITH RICE

350 g (12 oz) long green beans
1 teaspoon salt
1 tablespoon + 3 tablespoons oil
1.5 litres (52 fl oz) boiling water
4 cloves garlic, finely chopped
20 g (¾ oz) fresh ginger, finely chopped
¼ small brown onion, thinly sliced
1 tablespoon chilli flakes or 2 small fresh chillis, finely chopped
3 tablespoons preserved olive vegetable (optional)
30 g (1 oz) dried Chinese preserved olives, roughly chopped (optional)

Seasoning
1 teaspoon salt
1 teaspoon sugar
2 teaspoons soy sauce
pinch of white pepper
½ cube chicken bouillon powder (optional)

FRAGRANT SAUCY EGGPLANT

Eggplant is a great carrier of flavour and, when cooked until tender, it's unctuous and creamy. This dish is inspired by the classic Chinese flavour combination known as 'fish fragrant' — although there's no fish in the dish, it is said that the combination of soy sauce, sugar and black vinegar brings out a flavour that's reminiscent of seafood. I personally don't agree with this, I just think this flavour blend is pure pleasure on the palate. A simple yet flavourful dish that is surely a crowd-pleaser.

SERVES 2–4 AS A VEGE SIDE WITH RICE

2 large eggplant (approx. 600 g/1 lb 5 oz)
1 tablespoon salt
oil for deep-frying (approx. 400 ml/14 fl oz) + 3 tablespoons oil
1 tablespoon finely chopped ginger
3 cloves garlic, finely chopped
¼ brown onion, diced
100 ml (3½ fl oz) water
2 teaspoons cornflour mixed with 1 tablespoon water to make a thickening slurry
2 spring onions, sliced diagonally
coriander to garnish (optional)

Seasoning

2 teaspoons salt
1 tablespoon sugar
¼ teaspoon white pepper
1 tablespoon light soy sauce
1 teaspoon dark soy sauce
3 tablespoons black vinegar

Remove the stems and cut the eggplant into batons (or large chunks) approx 6 cm x 3 cm (2½ in x 1¼ in). Toss them with the salt in a large colander and leave for at least 30 minutes to drain.

In a wok or medium-sized pot, heat the oil for deep-frying to 180°C (350°F) and fry the eggplant in batches. The pieces should be soft yet holding their structure (approx. 3 minutes). Set aside. Pour the oil into a container to save for future cooks.

In a clean wok or pan, heat the 3 tablespoons oil over a high heat and fry the ginger, garlic and brown onion until aromatic (approx. 30 seconds). Add the seasoning and water. Once everything comes up to a simmer, add the eggplant and cook through for 5 minutes.

Slowly stir in as much of the slurry as needed to reach your desired consistency — it should resemble a thick pouring gravy.

Turn off the heat and stir in the spring onion. Taste and adjust seasoning if required.

Arrange the eggplant on a serving plate and garnish with coriander, if using.

THE LOWDOWN

Cut and salt the eggplant, allow to drain. Fry the eggplant in batches and reserve. In a pan/wok fry aromatics and eggplant with seasoning, thicken with slurry and garnish. Approx. 15 minutes, with 30 minutes salting time for eggplant.

PORK-STUFFED PEPPERS WITH SOY GRAVY

Pork-mince stuffed peppers are a Chinese classic, with many regional variations. The use of fatty pork mince to make vegetables go further is very common, especially in southern Chinese cuisine. Mince is affordable and when seasoned well it can make bland-tasting things exciting! This recipe only requires a small amount of meat to make capsicums taste incredible.

SERVES 2-4 AS A SIDE WITH RICE

Pork
- 300 g (10½ oz) pork mince (20 per cent fat ideally)
- 3 garlic cloves, minced
- 20 g (¾ oz) fresh ginger, minced
- 2 teaspoons salt
- 1 tablespoon sugar
- 1 teaspoon chicken bouillon powder (optional)
- ¼ teaspoon white pepper
- 2 teaspoons cornflour
- ¼ teaspoon fresh cracked black pepper
- 1 egg

Capsicums
- 400–500 g (14 oz–1 lb 2 oz) small to medium capsicums
- 1 tablespoon oil

Soy gravy
- 2 teaspoons cornflour
- 1 teaspoon chicken bouillon powder (optional)
- ½ teaspoon salt
- 2 teaspoons sugar
- 1 teaspoon dark soy
- 1 tablespoon light soy sauce
- 150 g (5½ fl oz) water

For the pork, place all the ingredients in a bowl and, using your hands or chopsticks, mix well in a circular motion until well combined and it reaches a gluey, thick texture (approx. 2–3 minutes). Set aside.

Prepare the capsicums by cutting each one in half top to bottom and removing the stalks and seeds. Depending on the size, you might need to cut them into quarters or into six segments — aim for sizes no bigger than 7 cm x 4 cm (2¾ in x 1½ in) each piece.

Stuff 1–2 tablespoons of the meat mix into each segment.

In a large/medium pan, heat the oil, add the stuffed capsicums and cover. Fry over a medium-high heat for 3 minutes on each side — there should be slight browning and caramelisation on the meat side. If your pan will not fit all the capsicums, fry in batches. If your capsicums are very thick, you may need to cook them for longer, with the lid on.

Place the cooked capsicums in a serving dish. Reserve the pan with the cooking juices.

Place all the ingredients for the gravy in a bowl/jug and mix well. Pour into the pan with the cooking juices and reduce until thickened over a medium-low heat (approx. 2 minutes).

Pour the gravy over the cooked capsicums and garnish with coriander if desired.

THE LOWDOWN

Mix the mince and seasoning together and stuff into cut capsicums. Pan-fry and add gravy ingredients. Approx. 25 minutes.

SPICY SAUCY TOFU

Inspired by the dish Ma Po Tofu, this spicy and saucy version is one of my favourite ways to prepare tofu. The fermented chilli combined with the Chinese 'trinity' of onion, garlic and ginger make it incredibly delicious to eat with bowls and bowls of plain white rice.

The recipe can be easily made vegan by removing the meat component and it's still just as delicious. It is preferable to use soft tofu, but other kinds will work too.

Place cubed tofu in a large, heatproof bowl and gently pour over a kettle of boiled water (approx 1.2 litres/43 fl oz) to heat and remove the raw flavour from the tofu. Let it sit for 10 minutes.

Meanwhile, in a large pan/wok add the oil, chilli bean paste, chilli flakes and fermented black bean and bring it up to a medium temperature, constantly moving the ingredients around to infuse the flavour into the oil (approx. 2 minutes).

Increase the heat to high and add the beef mince, ginger and garlic and cook for 5 minutes, using a spatula to break up the mince, until the meat is cooked through.

Drain the tofu in a colander in the sink (very carefully, as it's very soft) and gently transfer into the pan/wok, or use a slotted spoon to gently drain and transfer. Add the stock/water, white pepper and sugar and bring to a gentle simmer for a few minutes, stirring very gently and being careful not to break up the tofu.

Add the spring onion whites. Slowly stir in as much of the slurry as needed to reach your desired consistency — it should resemble a thick pouring gravy. Taste and adjust seasoning if needed.

Serve in a large bowl with the spring onion greens and the Sichuan pepper powder sprinkled over the top.

THE LOWDOWN

Pour boiling water over the tofu in a bowl to precook. Fry the aromatics in oil until fragrant, and then the beef until cooked through. Strain the tofu and gently mix into the beef. Thicken with slurry and garnish. Approx. 30 minutes.

SERVES 2-4 AS A VEGE SIDE WITH RICE

- 400–500 g (14 oz–1 lb 2 oz) soft tofu, drained and cut into 2 cm (¾ in) cubes
- ⅓ cup oil
- 1½ tablespoons fermented chilli bean paste (Sichuan style or Korean)
- 1 teaspoon chilli flakes
- 2 tablespoons fermented black bean
- 200 g (7 oz) minced beef (optional)
- 20 g (¾ oz) fresh ginger, finely chopped
- 4 cloves garlic, minced
- ½ cup stock or water
- ¼ teaspoon white pepper
- 1 teaspoon sugar
- 3 spring onions, greens and whites chopped separately
- 2 teaspoons cornflour mixed with 2 tablespoons water to make a thickening slurry
- pinch of Sichuan peppercorn powder (optional)

SALT AND PEPPER FRIED TOFU

Fried tofu is a gateway method of preparation for most people to get into the wonderful world of tofu. The crispy outer layer tossed in a special seasoning is giving fried chicken pleasure, without nearly as much of the guilt attached. It's the perfect dish for vegetarians or as something to accompany another protein so the table feels more balanced. One of the must-haves at the dinner table and an easy crowd-pleaser.

In a heatproof bowl, add the cubed tofu, salt and boiling water and leave to soak for 5 minutes. This will season the tofu. Drain the cubes of tofu in a colander then carefully lay them on a clean tea towel. Pat with paper towels until thoroughly dried.

Preheat the oil in a shallow non-stick pot and bring it up to 170ºC (325ºF). Place the tofu in a bowl, pour over the beaten egg and lightly toss until well coated. Sprinkle in the cornflour and coat all the pieces well. Fry in small batches (or all at once if using a large pan/pot) for 4-5 minutes, or until golden brown on the exterior. Take the tofu out with a slotted spoon or spider and set aside.

In a large pan/wok heat the 2 tablespoons of oil, then add the spring onion, garlic and capsicum and fry over a high heat for 1 minute until fragrant. Add the fried tofu cubes and stir-fry for 30 more seconds. Turn off the heat and sprinkle over all the seasonings and chilli, stirring well until combined.

Serve garnished with coriander, if using.

THE LOWDOWN

Pour boiling water and salt over the cubed tofu in a bowl, drain and dry. Coat with batter mix and fry until golden. Fry the aromatics in a pan and toss in the fried tofu. Garnish. Approx. 20–30 minutes.

SERVES 2-4 AS A VEGE SIDE WITH RICE

Tofu preparation
500 g (1 lb 2 oz) firm tofu, drained and cut into 3 cm (1¼ in) cubes
2 teaspoons salt
1 litre (35 fl oz) boiling water
500 ml (17 fl oz) canola or vegetable oil
1 egg, beaten
⅔ cup cornflour

Finishing
2 tablespoons oil
2 spring onions, chopped
3 cloves garlic, finely chopped
1 capsicum, deseeded and chopped into 1 cm (½ in) pieces
¼ teaspoon garlic powder
¼ teaspoon white pepper
½ teaspoon salt
1 teaspoon sugar
½ teaspoon chicken bouillon powder (optional)
1 red chilli, finely diced (optional)
coriander to garnish (optional)

TOMATO EGG

Along with instant noodles and congee. Chinese-style tomato egg is one of my first food memories growing up. It's a special dish that helped me foster this obsession with things that 'shouldn't work together but do'. It's beautiful I think, mainly because of how easy it is to like, almost in a guilty-pleasure kind of way — not just to me but a lot of my peers who have had a similar upbringing, fellow east Asians who grew up here in New Zealand.

The combination of savoury, tangy tomatoes with the soft and luxurious scrambled eggs makes it super umami, sweet and balanced. Here is my version of this incredibly easy, fast and simple vegetarian dish.

In a bowl, beat the eggs with 2 tablespoons sugar until mixed well. Chopsticks work well for this. Heat the ¼ cup of oil in a wok or large pan over a medium-high heat, pour in the eggs and give them a good mix with a spatula to scramble them. Turn off the heat after 10-20 seconds of cooking the eggs — they should look slightly runny and not quite cooked through. Remove the eggs and set aside.

Wipe the pan/wok clean with a paper towel and bring the heat back up to medium-high. Add the remaining 2 tablespoons oil and fry the onion, garlic and ginger for 2 minutes until fragrant. Add the tomatoes, salt, white pepper, chicken bouillon powder, if using, and the 1 tablespoon sugar. Cook until the tomatoes are softened but not mushy — the edges of the tomato wedges should be breaking but still holding shape (approx. 4 minutes). Taste and adjust at this point if need be. It should be slightly salty because the sweet eggs later will balance it out.

Pour in the slurry and stir the tomatoes until thickened and the liquids in the pan/wok have reduced a little.

Turn off the heat and gently stir in the eggs for 30 seconds — the residual heat from the pan will finish cooking the eggs. Garnish with spring onion greens, if using.

SERVES 2-4 AS A SIDE WITH RICE

6 large eggs
2 tablespoons + 1 tablespoon white sugar
¼ cup + 2 tablespoons oil
¼ brown onion, sliced
2 cloves garlic, smacked
5 g (⅛ oz) fresh ginger, thinly sliced
3 medium tomatoes (approx 400 g/14 oz), stems removed and each cut into 6 wedges
2 teaspoons salt
¼ teaspoon white pepper
1 teaspoon chicken bouillon powder (optional)
1 teaspoon cornflour mixed with 1 tablespoon water to make a thickening slurry
small handful of spring onion greens to garnish (optional)

THE LOWDOWN

Soft-scramble eggs and sugar in a pan with oil and set aside. Fry aromatics with tomato and season. Stir eggs back into pan and thicken with slurry. Approx. 15 minutes.

TEA-SOAKED SOY EGGS

This makes an excellent cold side dish. Keep the soaking liquid in a container in the fridge (for a few weeks) or freezer (for 3 months) to make more tea eggs in the future — just boil more eggs to soak in the broth. Make sure to reboil the broth before using every time — it may need more seasoning.

In a medium pot, cook the eggs for 9 minutes in enough boiling water to submerge the eggs. Take out the eggs and cool in a bowl of cold water until warm to the touch (approx 10 minutes).

Using the back of a spoon, hit the shells until cracked all around, keeping the shells on for the marbling effect. Set aside.

Place all the other ingredients in a medium-sized pot with 800 ml (28 fl oz) water and bring to a low simmer with the lid on. Simmer for 15 minutes so the spices become infused with the water. Taste to see if it's salty enough. Add more salt if need be (it should be a very saline solution). Turn off heat.

Place eggs in the hot broth and leave to to marinate overnight. Peel and enjoy. Best eaten from day 2-4.

MAKES 10

10 eggs
800 ml (28 fl oz) water
5 tea bags
1 teaspoon five-spice powder
5 star anise
1 teaspoon black peppercorns
4 bay leaves
¾ cup light soy sauce
3 tablespoons salt
½ cup dark soy sauce
½ cup sugar
3 garlic cloves, smacked
20 g (¾ oz) fresh ginger, thinly sliced

THE LOWDOWN

Boil whole eggs for 9 minutes, cool slightly and smack the shells. Boil spices, seasoning and tea leaves with water and soak the eggs overnight or longer. Approx. 20 minutes plus overnight soaking.

BASIC STEAMED EGGS

Steamed eggs hold a strong nostalgic memory for me — I believe it is the first type of egg dish I ate as a baby because of how soft and creamy it is. As I get older that desire to eat perfectly steamed egg hasn't gone away, except now I like to add toppings such as seafood or minced meat to please my slightly more sophisticated palate.

SERVES 2-4 AS A SIDE WITH RICE

200 ml (7 fl oz) hot water
5 eggs (size 6)
1 teaspoon salt
2 teaspoons sugar
pinch of white pepper
½ teaspoon sesame oil
2 teaspoons light soy sauce
chopped coriander or spring onion to garnish (optional)

Set a steamer over a wok/large pot filled with at least 2 litres (70 fl oz) of water over a high heat.

To make the egg mix, start by heating 200 ml (7 fl oz) water to about 60°C (140°F), using a thermometer to measure it if you have one or go by if it's too hot to touch for more than 3 seconds.

Crack the eggs into a bowl and use chopsticks to whisk well. Slowly whisk in the hot water until combined. Then whisk in the salt, sugar and pepper and pour into a steamproof bowl/dish (ceramic or stainless steel dishes work best).

Steam on high for the first 5 minutes, then turn the heat to medium and continue steaming until the egg is just cooked. To check the doneness of the egg, give it a gentle shake and if there is minimal wobble in the centre of the egg, it is done (I tend to take it out just before it's cooked so the residual heat will finish the cooking). Total steaming time is about 14-18 minutes, depending on the heat absorption of the bowl/dish used. The egg is perfect if there are no air bubbles or cracks.

The egg can be eaten topped with sesame oil, light soy sauce and coriander/spring onion, or try it with one of the topping/variations suggestions over the page.

THE LOWDOWN

Mix eggs with hot water and seasoning. Pour mixture into a dish for steaming. Steam until eggs are cooked, serve plain or with toppings. Approx. 20 minutes.

BASIC STEAMED EGGS: TOPPING SUGGESTIONS

Scallops in gravy

Heat the oil in a small saucepan over a medium heat. Add the scallops, garlic and ginger and fry for 30 seconds (try not to let the scallops brown). Add the water/stock and the seasonings and bring to a simmer. Once the scallops are almost cooked through, pink in the middle with a slight bounce when pushed with your finger (approx. 3 minutes), slowly stir in as much of the slurry as needed to reach your desired consistency — the sauce should resemble a thick pouring gravy. Pour over the steamed egg base and garnish with coriander if using.

THE LOWDOWN

In a pan, fry the scallops and aromatics, add the liquid and thicken with slurry. Pour over steamed eggs. Approx. 5 minutes.

- 1 tablespoon oil
- 250 g (9 oz) scallops (frozen or fresh)
- 1 clove garlic, chopped
- 5 g (⅛ oz) fresh ginger, finely chopped
- 100 g (3½ fl oz) water or stock
- 1 teaspoon chicken bouillon powder
- ½ teaspoon salt
- ¼ teaspoon white pepper
- 1 teaspoon sugar
- ¾ teaspoon cornflour mixed with 2 tablespoons water to make a thickening slurry
- coriander to garnish (optional)

Pork or chicken mince

The difference in this version is adding marinated pork or chicken to the egg mix before steaming. It's a great way to use up leftover dumpling/wonton filling too (a good reminder that you might have some frozen in your freezer already?).

Mix the ingredients in a small bowl until combined and sticky, about 3 minutes. Dip a teaspoon into a small bowl of cold water (to prevent the mixture sticking to the spoon) and use it to scoop up the meat mixture. Plop little bits of the mince mix all over the egg mix in the dish before steaming.

Steam as you would normally, making sure the meat is cooked through. Total steam time 16-20 minutes.

THE LOWDOWN

Mix the meat with seasoning, scoop bits onto the egg mix before steaming. Steam approx. 20 minutes.

- 100 g (3½ oz) chicken or pork mince (the higher the fat content the better)
- ½ teaspoon salt
- 1 teaspoon chicken bouillon powder
- 1 teaspoon sugar
- pinch of white pepper
- ½ teaspoon cornflour
- 1 tablespoon water

Soy shiitake gravy

Heat the oil to a high heat in a small pot or pan. Add the mushrooms, spring onion, garlic and ginger and cook, stirring constantly, for 3 minutes, until aromatic and the mushrooms have lost some moisture. Add the water/stock, salt, sugar, pepper, light and dark soy, black vinegar and bouillon powder, if using. Bring everything to a simmer and cook for a further 5 minutes over a medium heat. Slowly stir in as much of the slurry as needed to reach your desired consistency — the sauce should resemble a thick pouring gravy. Pour over the steamed egg base.

1 tablespoon oil

150 g (5½ oz) fresh shiitake mushrooms, thinly sliced (rehydrated dried shiitake work well too)

30 g (1 oz) finely chopped spring onion

2 cloves garlic, finely chopped

10 g (¼ oz) fresh ginger, finely chopped

200 ml (7 fl oz) water or stock

1 teaspoon salt

1 tablespoon sugar

pinch of white pepper

1 teaspoon dark soy sauce

1 tablespoon light soy sauce

2 teaspoons black vinegar

1 teaspoon chicken bouillon powder or mushroom/vege stock powder (optional)

1½ teaspoons cornflour mixed with 2 tablespoons water to make a thickening slurry

THE LOWDOWN

Fry the mushrooms and aromatics, add the liquid and seasonings and thicken with slurry. Pour over the steamed eggs. Approx. 10 minutes.

CHINESE CHIVE OMELETTE

These home-style egg omelettes are something you'd mostly come across only in Chinese households, as they are not commonly found in restaurants. The simple yet delicious nature of fried eggs is a great carrier of flavour, and they work with almost any filling options, whether it be a vegetable or protein.

In a wok/large fry pan heat 1 teaspoon of oil until hot, add the chopped chives (or spring onion) and a pinch of salt and fry over a high heat for 2 minutes, or until softened. Remove and place in a mixing bowl.

Add the remaining ingredients to the bowl, except the ¼ cup oil. Whisk the eggs and mix everything until well combined. The cornflour will stop the water from separating from the eggs during the cooking, giving you a creamy, softer egg texture.

Reheat the wok/fry pan until hot and add the ¼ cup oil. It seems like a lot but you want the outside of the egg to brown up and crisp nicely. When the oil is hot, reduce the heat to medium and pour in the egg mixture. Allow the eggs to fry and brown up a little, using a spatula to move and slightly scramble the eggs but not too much, as you're trying to keep it in one piece.

After 2-3 minutes, try to flip the omelette or break it into sections like pizza with the spatula and flip the sections. Brown the other side (another 1-2 minutes) and it's done.

SERVES 2-4 AS A SIDE WITH RICE

1 teaspoon + ¼ cup oil

100 g (3½ oz) Chinese chives, chopped into 1 cm (½ in) lengths or substitute with spring onion

pinch of salt

6 eggs

1 tablespoon cornflour mixed with 1 tablespoon water

pinch of white pepper

1 teaspoon salt

1 teaspoon sugar

THE LOWDOWN

Fry the chives or spring onions in a pan and add to a bowl with eggs, seasonings and cornflour mix. Fry the omelette on both sides. Approx. 10 minutes.

OYSTER OMELETTE

Here is another variation I grew up eating. Pro tip: serve these with your favourite chilli oil and a dollop of mayonnaise — you won't regret it!

Place the raw oysters in a strainer or colander over the sink. Pour some freshly boiled water from the kettle over the oysters to remove impurities and to slightly precook them. This takes only 5–10 seconds — you want them still raw on the inside. Shake dry and place in a mixing bowl.

Add the remaining ingredients, except for the oil. Whisk the eggs and mix everything until well combined. The cornflour will stop the water from separating from the eggs during the cooking, giving you a creamy, softer egg texture.

Heat a wok/large fry pan until hot and add the oil. It seems like a lot but you want the outside of the egg to brown up and crisp nicely. When the oil is hot, reduce the heat to medium and pour in the egg mixture. Allow the eggs to fry and brown up a little, using a spatula to move and slightly scramble the eggs but not too much, as you're trying to keep it in one piece.

After 2–3 minutes, try to flip the omelette or break it into sections like pizza with a spatula and flip the sections. Brown the other side (another 1–2 minutes) and it's done.

SERVES 2–4 AS A SIDE WITH RICE

200 g (7 oz) oysters (fresh or thawed frozen)
5 eggs
1 spring onion, thinly sliced
1 tablespoon cornflour mixed with 1 tablespoon water
pinch of white pepper
1 teaspoon salt
1 teaspoon sugar
¼ cup oil

THE LOWDOWN

Pour boiling water over oysters and add to the bowl with eggs and seasoning. Mix, then fry the egg mix on both sides. Approx. 10 minutes.

RICE & NOODLES

PLAIN RICE

This is perhaps one of two ingredients I have consumed the most in my lifetime (coffee being the other) and is a staple in my diet. Growing up in a Cantonese household the main carbohydrate was rice, whereas it's wheat in the north part of China, where noodles and dumplings are the heroes.

This book is mostly designed around food that is eaten with plain white rice, so protein and vege dishes are served in the middle of the table and each person gets a rice bowl.

Many different factors come into play when cooking 'perfect' rice — the rice type used, the type of pot, the heat source and so on . . .

Here is a guide to how I cook rice in a rice cooker or on a stovetop. After cooking it the first time, you should be able to find out if it needs tweaks to make it better the next time, maybe with more or less water etc. P.S. I highly recommend a rice cooker as it just makes life so much easier!

My ideal ratio is roughly one part rice to two parts water. Allow roughly ½–¾ cup raw rice per person.

Rinse the rice in a bowl or colander until the water runs almost clear (this removes excess starch).

If using the stove, in a pot with the rinsed rice add the water and bring to a boil over a medium-high heat. When it boils, turn the heat down to the lowest setting, cover, and simmer for 14-16 minutes. Turn off the heat and allow it to continue cooking in its own heat for at least 10-15 minutes. Fluff the rice with a non-stick scoop before serving.

If using a rice cooker, add the rinsed rice and water to the cooker and switch on to cook. The switch should flip up when done. Allow the rice to rest for at least 10 minutes and fluff it before serving.

SERVES 4-6

3 cups white jasmine long-grain rice (or your favourite)
1.1–1.2 litres (39–43 fl oz) water

THE LOWDOWN

Add rinsed rice to pot/rice cooker with water. Bring to a simmer and wait. Approx. 30 minutes.

CANTONESE CONGEE

Nothing beats a warming and nourishing pot of Cantonese-style congee (thick savoury rice porridge), served as is or with your favourite toppings or as is, to give you the feeling that everything's gonna be okay. Congee is one of my all-time favourite comfort foods and perhaps one of my most significant food memories.

It was originally created a few thousand years ago in India to make grains go further — so much further, to a point where you can serve up to four people with one cup of rice!

Congee is eaten for breakfast or lunch in most east Asian countries, and for many it's the equivalent of the West's chicken noodle soup — when someone is not feeling their best, this is what you serve.

Congee is great stored as leftovers.

Put the rice in a bowl, rinse the grains well and empty out the water, or rinse with running water in a sieve under the tap until water runs almost clear (2 minutes).

In a large pot, add the oil, ginger and garlic and fry, moving it around with a spatula over a medium heat for 45 seconds, or until aromatic. You don't want to colour the aromatics.

Add the rinsed rice, salt, sugar and water. Bring to a gentle boil then reduce the heat to a low simmer, stirring gently every few minutes (make sure you scrape the bottom) until the rice thickens to a really thick, gravy-type consistency. This will take 30-45 minutes depending on rice type.

Once the rice is at the consistency you desire, turn off the heat. At this point you can water it down to loosen the congee if it's too thick, making sure it's brought back up to a gentle boil again if you do.

This is a simple base that is perfect to build on if you want to add marinated protein, or serve as is with your favourite toppings.

Great toppings include: century egg (cut into small dice), fried shallots, homemade chilli oil, Chinese fried bread (youtiao), pickled greens, onsen egg (an egg that's been cooked to 60°C [140°F]), soft-boiled egg, sliced spring onion or pork floss.

THE LOWDOWN

Boil the rice and water with the seasonings until thick and creamy. Approx. 1 hour.

RATIO: 1 PART RICE TO 12 PARTS WATER
SERVES 4-5

1 cup rice of your choice
2 tablespoons oil
30 g (1 oz) fresh ginger, minced
2 cloves garlic, minced
1 tablespoon salt
2 tablespoons sugar
approx. 2.5 litres (88 fl oz) water

Chicken congee

In a bowl, marinate the chicken with all the other ingredients for at least 30 minutes. When the congee base is cooked to your desired consistency, add the marinated chicken and stir through (the chicken will cook in a few minutes). Cook for a further 1-2 minutes and turn off the heat. The residual heat will finish the cooking without drying the chicken out.

THE LOWDOWN

Marinate the chicken and stir through the hot congee until cooked.

FOR 1 CUP RICE CONGEE BATCH

300 g (10½ oz) chicken cut into 1 cm (½ in) cubes (skinless, boneless chicken thigh or breast)
2 teaspoons salt
1 teaspoon chicken bouillon powder (optional)
1 tablespoon cornflour
⅓ teaspoon white pepper
1 tablespoon rice wine
10 g (¼ oz) fresh ginger, minced

Fish congee

In a bowl, marinate the sliced fish strips with all the other ingredients for at least 15 minutes. When the congee base is cooked to your desired consistency, turn off the heat. Add the marinated fish to the congee base and gently stir through, trying not to break the fish up. The residual heat will cook the fish and have it remain tender.

THE LOWDOWN

Marinate the fish and stir through the hot congee until cooked.

FOR 1 CUP RICE CONGEE BATCH

400 g (14 oz) skinless, boned fish fillet, cut into strips about 5 mm (¼ in) thick (thawed frozen basa or any white fish works well)
1 teaspoon salt
2 teaspoons sugar
1 tablespoon cornflour
⅓ teaspoon white pepper
1 tablespoon rice wine
10 g (¼ oz) fresh ginger, minced

Pork and century egg congee

In a bowl, marinate the cubed pork pieces with all the seasonings and leave for at least an hour or overnight in the fridge.

As the rice and water start to boil when making the congee base, add the pork and gently stir through. The pork will need at least 30 minutes' cooking time and will easily be broken up into small pieces throughout the congee. When at the desired congee texture, stir in the century egg and serve immediately.

FOR 1 CUP RICE CONGEE BASE

300 g (10½ oz) pork, skinless, cut into small (3 cm (1¼ in) cubes
1 tablespoon salt
2 teaspoons sugar
1½ tablespoons cornflour
⅓ teaspoon white pepper
1 tablespoon rice wine
20 g (¾ oz) fresh ginger, minced
2 century eggs, shelled and cut into 5 mm (¼ in) cubes

THE LOWDOWN

Marinate the pork and cook with the rice until failing into pieces. Add century egg and stir through.

TOMATO AND FERMENTED CABBAGE OMELETTE RICE

I have a vivid memory of eating fried rice with tomato sauce and fried eggs as a kid. I was about five years old and would have this at my parents' cafe in Nausori, Fiji, where I would eat it off bright blue plastic plates. Tomato, rice and eggs are a combo you don't really think of, but it works and it's a beautiful thing.

For the tomato rice, heat the oil in a fry pan/wok over a high heat, add the onion, garlic and ginger and fry for 30 seconds. Add the fermented cabbage, tomato and tomato sauce and cook about 5 minutes. Add the seasoning and stir through the rice until coated. Taste and adjust if need be. Continue stir-frying the rice until it is hot, approx. 3–5 minutes.

For the omelette, crack the eggs in a bowl with the other ingredients except the oil and whisk/mix the ingredients well. Heat a small non-stick pan to medium-low heat with the oil, pour in the egg mixture and start scrambling by agitating the egg in circular movements with chopsticks or a spatula until about 60 per cent cooked — runny on top and cooked underneath but not browned. Turn the heat to low and slowly and carefully roll the egg into an oval shape by tilting the pan away from you and using the chopsticks/spatula to aid in flipping/rolling the egg towards you. Flicking the pan towards you while using the chopsticks to roll helps here. About 3 or 4 flips should create the ideal shape. The tomato rice serves 2 so if necessary make a second omelette (or you can keep the second portion of tomato rice to eat another day).

Spoon the desired amount of rice onto the plate and carefully lay the egg on top of the rice. Before serving, cut the egg open by running a knife over the top so the gooey middle flows over the rice. Serve with extra tomato sauce and fermented cabbage (or kimchi) if desired.

THE LOWDOWN

Fry aromatics in oil, add fermented cabbage and seasonings, add cooked rice and heat through. Whisk egg with seasoning and fry in a pan, shaping it into an oval with the inside being a soft scramble. Place over rice. Approx. 20 minutes.

SERVES 2

Tomato rice
3 tablespoons oil
½ small white onion, diced
2 cloves garlic, minced
10 g (¼ oz) fresh ginger, minced
100 g (3½ oz) Beancurd Fermented Chinese Cabbage (see page 40), diced, or store-bought kimchi, diced
1 medium ripe tomato, diced, or ⅓ cup canned diced tomato
½ cup tomato sauce
2 tablespoons light soy sauce
salt and white pepper to taste
1 tablespoon sugar
2 cups cooked rice (leftovers are perfect)

Omelette (makes 1)
3 eggs
1 teaspoon salt
2 teaspoons sugar
2 tablespoons oil

SPAM FRIED RICE

I love Spam! I always find it bizarre when people I encounter show their dislike of it. It's almost like a first-date red-flag reaction where I feel the need to prove them wrong. Perhaps they dislike it because of the way it has been prepared for them, or is a toxic ex attached to that particular food memory? Either way I'll defend Spam until the day I die. It's a weird flex.

This recipe is a perfect way to use up your leftover rice and to crack open that can of Spam in the back of your pantry. For me this is a dish filled with childhood nostalgia — the perfect combination of the salty, fatty flavours of the Spam with the sweet, eggy garlic rice.

If you're not a fan of Spam or want an alternative protein, Chinese dried sausage (lap cheong) is a great substitute as it adds a beautiful sweet flavour to the dish. Simply slice the sausage into really thin slices like coins and treat it the same as the Spam in this recipe.

In a heated medium-sized pan/wok, fry the Spam over medium-high heat until browned on most sides (about 3 minutes). Take out the Spam and set aside.

Keep the pan over the same heat and add the oil. Crack in the eggs and use a spatula to move the eggs around to scramble and break them up for 1 minute. Add the garlic and onion and cook for a further minute until aromatic and the onions begin to look transparent.

Loosen the rice before adding it to the pan by breaking it up with your fingers or a fork. Add the rice with the Spam and seasoning and stir-fry until hot and mixed through, about 5 minutes.

SERVES 2

½ 340 g (12 oz) can Spam, cut into 1 cm (½ in) cubes
2 tablespoons oil
2 eggs
3 cloves garlic, minced
½ small onion, diced
2 cups cooked rice (leftovers are perfect)

Seasoning
1½ tablespoons sugar
1½ tablespoons light soy sauce
1 teaspoon salt
¼ teaspoon white pepper

THE LOWDOWN

Fry the Spam until brown and set aside. Scramble the eggs, aromatics and cooked rice with the seasonings. Add Spam and heat through. Approx. 15 minutes.

CREAMY PEANUT BUTTER NOODLES

This quick and easy flavour-packed creamy noodle dish is one of my guilty-pleasure dishes for one when I'm craving a carb-loaded, high-fat meal. It's one of those dishes that is often overlooked because of how easy it is to prepare.

This flavour combination of soy and nut butters or sesame paste is a common mix known as 'strange flavour' in Chinese cooking. When adapted to the great nut butter options available to us, it's a fun pick-your-own-adventure kinda dish, where you can have infinite combinations like soba with almond butter, or rice noodles with tahini. The world is your noodle and butter choice here!

You can get fresh wheat noodles from your local Asian grocer and you can easily increase the amount of ingredients to make as many serves as you want.

Start by boiling a pot of water for your noodles. Follow packet instructions for the ideal chewy, al dente texture. Fresh wheat noodles should take about 3-4 minutes to cook, so make sure to not overcook them. Reserve about ½ cup of the cooking liquid for the sauce.

Mix together the remaining ingredients. Add the reserved cooking water into the seasoning mix and whisk until a creamy sauce is formed. Taste and adjust if need be.

Strain the cooked noodles and mix into the sauce. Serve in a bowl topped with the garnishes. Chilli oil will give it an extra flavour explosion.

SERVES 1

200 g (7 oz) fresh wheat noodles (or a single serve of your favourite noodle without the seasoning packet)
60 g (2¼ oz) peanut butter or your favourite nut butter
2 teaspoons sugar
1½ tablespoons light soy sauce
2 teaspoons rice vinegar or white vinegar
1 clove garlic, minced

Garnish

½ spring onion green, sliced diagonally
1 teaspoon sesame seeds, toasted (optional)
Chilli oil (optional)

THE LOWDOWN

Cook noodles. Mix seasonings and cooking water to form a sauce. Stir through the noodles and garnish. Approx. 15 minutes.

Modern Chinese

QUICK AND EASY SPRING ONION OIL NOODLES

This quick noodle dish is unassumingly delicious: slippery from the aromatic spring onion-infused oil and when cooked perfectly the noodles will have a beautiful chewy texture to them.

This is a super simple dish that is a perfect base to build on — feel free to add your choice of protein.

Bring a medium/large pot of water to the boil.

Heat the oil in a wok/pan over a medium-high heat. Add the spring onion whites and fry, moving them around the pan to avoid burning, for 2 minutes until softened. Add in the garlic and spring onion greens and stir-fry for about 2 minutes. Add in the seasoning and cook for a further 1 minute. Turn off the heat.

Cook the noodles according to the packet instructions — but they should still be chewy. Use a spider to remove the noodles from the water or drain them through a colander, and shake off excess water. Throw the noodles into the oil sauce and stir-fry until thoroughly mixed for about 1 minute on high heat. Garnish if desired.

SERVES 1

⅓ cup oil

2 spring onions, greens and whites cut into 3 cm (1¼ in) lengths separately

2 cloves garlic, thinly sliced

200 g (7 oz) wheat or egg noodles or noodle of your choice (ideally something with bite)

½ teaspoon chilli flakes to garnish (optional)

toasted sesame seeds to garnish (optional)

Seasoning

2 tablespoons light soy sauce

1 tablespoon dark soy sauce

1 tablespoon sugar

½ teaspoon salt

THE LOWDOWN

Boil the noodles. Fry the aromatics in oil and seasoning, toss the cooked noodles together with the seasonings and garnish. Approx. 10–15 minutes.

SAUCY DAN DAN NOODLES

A very popular Sichuan street-food noodle snack from central China, this dish has become hugely popular around the world with the rise of Sichuan and regional Chinese restaurants in the West. With its unique taste it's a great representation of signature flavours from the central part of China — the combination of fragrant chilli oil and 'strange flavour' sauce makes this dish one that entices the whole palate. Dan dan refers to the poles that street-food vendors use to carry the noodles and bowls on their shoulders when hitting the streets. Lucky for you, here's my version for you to make in the comfort of your own home.

I often use the noodle-blanching water to cook some greens, such as bok choy or broccoli, to serve alongside the dish for a more balanced meal.

For the sauce, mix all the ingredients in a bowl and set aside.

For the meat, in a preheated wok/fry pan add the oil, mince and fermented mustard green and fry over a high heat for 30 seconds. Add the remaining ingredients and use a ladle to press down on the mince to break the bits up. Stir-fry until the mince is cooked through, about 5 minutes. Turn off the heat and set aside.

Cook the noodles according to packet instructions. For most fresh wheat noodles about 2-3 minutes will be perfect, as you still want to retain some chew.

Strain, shaking off the excess liquid. Divide the noodles among bowls and spoon 3-4 tablespoons of the sauce over each and some of the cooked mince. Garnish with spring onion and sesame seeds. Stir the sauce and mince thoroughly before eating.

For a vegetarian option, swap out the meat for 150 g (5½ oz) finely diced fresh shiitake mushrooms and increase the amount of fermented mustard green to 100 g (3½ oz), reduce the amount of salt used as the mustard green is quite salty. Stir-fry as above for the mince.

SERVES 3-4

Sauce

⅓ cup Chinese sesame paste (or tahini or your favourite nut butter)

1 tablespoon dark soy sauce

¼ cup light soy sauce

1 tablespoon sugar

3 tablespoons black vinegar or rice vinegar or white vinegar

¼ cup chilli oil (with sediment)

3 tablespoons water to thin out the sauce

Meat

2 tablespoons oil

200 g (7 oz) pork mince (or beef or lamb mince)

3 tablespoons preserved mustard green (ya cai) or kimchi, finely chopped (optional)

Ingredients continued on opposite page

1 tablespoon rice wine
1 teaspoon salt
1 tablespoon light soy sauce
5 cloves garlic, minced
¼ teaspoon white pepper
pinch of toasted ground Sichuan pepper (optional)

To assemble
200 g (7 oz) fresh wheat noodles per person (or substitute with your favourite noodles, dried work well too)
spring onion, thinly sliced, to garnish
toasted sesame seeds, to garnish (optional)

THE LOWDOWN

Mix the sauce ingredients. Stir-fry mince with aromatics until cooked. Cook your favourite noodles and strain. Place the noodles, sauce and mince in a bowl. Garnish, mix and enjoy! Approx. 30–40 minutes.

Because There Are Things We Cannot Say
(Mum, I am gay.)

During those early mother meals

Steamed egg is just steamed egg

The sound of lips smacking

And ceramic clanging

Is a beginner's symphony

And you are not yet a picky eater

(I was born, but . . .)

Soon more bowls of rice are scooped

Over and over

One more bowl? she says

Mouth stuffed to fill the silence

Mouth stuffed

To keep you   longer

You cannot leave   until the last grain is gone

(I want to hang out with my friends.)

Pushing it aside

Nose turned   arms outstretched

Chopsticks stand tall   like two joss sticks

Stabbing bowl of the rice   like white dirt

Like calamity   like grief

And all you crave is cheeseburger

(I am going to be home late.)

Attempts are made
Spag bol	and	toasted sandwiches
She cosplays her cooking	to the likeness
Of your white friend's mother's
She has heard you yearning for their dishes
too often to ignore
(I need to move away.)

Because there are things we cannot say
When you finally come home she lays down
Your favourite dishes
Lines them up like apology
Orange slices cut up in the shape of
All those missing syllables
Like truce	after truce	after truce
(I am sorry. I am sorry. I am sorry.)

When you miss her	cooking
All you mutter over the phone is
How did you make	that?	*(ancestral vibes? you wonder.)*
But what you mean is . . .
*(How did you make	me?)*
(How did you know what I needed?)
(How have you always known?)

Nathan Joe
writer, performance poet and theatre-maker

SEAFOOD

VIBRANT SEAFOOD PROSPERITY SALAD

About three years ago, I was first introduced to Yee Sang Lo Hei, a vibrant salad traditionally enjoyed during Chinese New Year in many east Asian countries, especially Malaysia and Singapore. Yee sang translates to raw fish, and lo hei means elevated toss.

My friend Amanda is of Singaporean descent and would host a large gathering at her home during Chinese New Year, where the main activity would be to participate in the prosperous salad toss. The first time I attended one of these events, I was wondering why there was a set-up involving a separate trestle table and a tarp on the ground, indoors, for a salad. I soon realised that part of the ritual is to toss the salad as high as possible to wish for prosperity to the heights for the coming year. Almost like a food fight, but instead of throwing food at each other, you're flinging it up in the air wishing for luck, fortune and love, surrounded by people who want it as badly as you do. The tarp makes a lot of sense now.

My version of the prosperity salad has all the components of the traditional one but with some extra things so that it's just a generally yummy salad, balanced in flavour and texture to excite the palate. The homemade sauces and salmon roe for a pop of briny complexity make it a well-rounded salad that could be prepared not only for Chinese New Year, but any large group gathering.

For the fried wontons, heat the oil in a small pot to 170°C (325°F). Fry the wonton skins for 2-3 minutes until crispy and golden. Set aside.

For the plum sauce, place everything in a small pot and bring to a gentle simmer. Simmer on low for 15 minutes, stirring every few minutes to break down the fruit pieces, until the sauce has thickened. Strain the sauce through a sieve, using the back of a spoon to push through sediments, and allow it to cool. If you don't want to make your own sauce, substitute with ½ cup store-bought plum sauce mixed with 1 tablespoon soy sauce.

For the seasoning sauce, mix everything together well in a small bowl and set aside.

To assemble the salad, arrange all the prepped vegetables, fruit and tofu (if using) on a large serving platter in separate sections. Aim for high contrast in colours for a stunning presentation.

On separate dishes arrange the raw fish, sesame seeds, wonton skins and sauces so the ritual of tossing the salad can be done accordingly, with a lucky saying attached to every addition to the platter. The sayings will vary according to people's upbringing.

SERVES 8-10

Fried wontons

200 ml (7 fl oz) neutral oil
50 g (1¾ oz) wonton skins, cut into 1 cm x 4 cm (½ in x 1½ in) strips

Plum sauce

200 g (7 oz) ripe plums, deseeded and chopped
100 g (3½ oz) honey
50 g (1¾ oz) sugar
30 g (1 oz) fresh ginger, sliced
2 teaspoons salt
1 tablespoon soy sauce
100 g (3½ fl oz) water

Recipe and ingredients continued overleaf

½ teaspoon five-spice powder
2 star anise
1 cinnamon stick

Seasoning sauce
1 tablespoon yuzu kosho (yuzu chilli salt preserve)*
3 tablespoons apple cider vinegar
1 tablespoon caster sugar
1 teaspoon salt

*Yuzu kosho can be substituted with 1 small fresh chilli, chopped and mixed with the zest and juice of 1 lemon and 1 tablespoon salt

Salad
1 telegraph cucumber, deseeded and julienned
½ young daikon radish, peeled and julienned
¼ red cabbage, shredded
1 medium carrot, peeled and julienned
1 green capsicum, deseeded and thinly sliced
1 red capsicum, deseeded and thinly sliced
5 red radishes, thinly sliced
1 Asian pear, cored and julienned
4 limes, halved

300 g (10½ oz) salmon fillet, skinned, boned and thinly sliced
300 g (10½ oz) tuna fillet, thinly sliced
3 tablespoons sesame seeds, toasted
30 g (1 oz) coriander, roughly chopped

Optional add-ons
100 g (3½ oz) salmon roe
200 g (7 oz) marinated tofu, thinly sliced
100 g (3½ oz) store-bought yellow pickled daikon, julienned

Once the sayings are completed, all the ingredients and sauces and should be on the serving tray. This is when everyone at the table uses chopsticks to toss the salad together.

As they say, the higher the toss the more prosperous your new year will be, so prepare to get messy!

THE LOWDOWN

Fry wonton skins. Prepare the sauces — one is a simple mix of ingredients, the other is cooked-down plums with seasoning. Prep all the vegetables, tofu and fish and arrange on a large platter. Serve sauces separately and dress at the table before the toss. Ideally prepped the night before and stored in the fridge. Approx. 90 minutes.

STEAMED OYSTERS WITH VERMICELLI AND EXPLODED AROMATICS

This special dish is mostly eaten at Cantonese restaurants when there's a celebration or a banquet around the lazy susan.

It is a pretty costly dish to order when eating out, hence why it's a 'sometimes dish'. However, if you make it at home it's sure to impress any foodie and it's cost effective to produce. Oh yeah, the best part is that it can be all prepped way before dinner.

SERVES 4–6 AS A PROTEIN SIDE WITH RICE

Sauce

¼ cup light soy sauce
2 tablespoons sugar
¼ teaspoon white pepper

80 g (2¾ oz) dried fine rice vermicelli
1 litre (35 fl oz) boiling water
12–18 large Pacific oysters, shucked
40 g (1½ oz) fresh ginger, finely chopped
1 spring onion, finely chopped
6 cloves garlic, finely chopped
¼ cup oil
2 small fresh chillis, thinly sliced (optional)

For the sauce, place the ingredients in a bowl and microwave for 30 seconds or until the sugar is dissolved. Mix and set aside.

Soak the vermicelli in a bowl with the boiling water for a few minutes until the noodles have completely softened. Drain the hot water and refill with cold water to prevent the noodles from cooking further. Drain water and shake dry or leave in a colander to drain dry. Using scissors, snip the vermicelli into shorter lengths, about 4 cm (1½ in).

Bring a pot of water up to the boil for steaming (minimum 2 litres/70 fl oz). In a large steamer basket or multiple smaller ones, place a shallow bowl inside and arrange the oysters, trying to keep them upright so they don't tip their juices out when steamed.

Place a small bunch of the cut vermicelli over each one (about 1-2 tablespoons) and sprinkle the chopped ginger over them. Steam for 5-7 minutes or until the oysters are just cooked through. Remove oysters from the heat and place 1 teaspoon of sauce in each. Top with the spring onion and garlic.

In a small pot, heat the oil to about 220°C (400°F), or when a wooden chopstick bubbles when dunked into the oil. Pour or spoon the oil over the oysters, about 1 teaspoon in each. The oil should sizzle and release the aromas from the garlic and spring onion. Careful as the oil might splatter. Garnish with chilli.

THE LOWDOWN

Microwave sauce ingredients. Soak vermicelli in hot water, drain and snip shorter. Steam oysters with ginger and vermicelli on top. Add spring onion, garlic and sauce. Spoon hot oil over and garnish. Approx. 25 minutes.

STEAMED SALMON IN CHILLI BEAN SAUCE

This perfectly balanced combination of spicy, fragrant flavours and the delicate steamed salmon makes this an incredibly drool-worthy main for the middle of the table.

Substitute the salmon with any fish — frozen basa fillets work well too. Just be aware that steaming times will differ depending on the fish type, size and fat content. Feel free to use a whole fish instead.

SERVES 2-4 AS A PROTEIN SIDE WITH RICE

600–800 g (1 lb 5 oz–1 lb 12 oz) pin-boned, skin-on salmon fillets
2 tablespoons Shaoxing or any aromatic rice wine
½ teaspoon salt
30 g (1 oz) fresh ginger, sliced

Chilli sauce

3 tablespoons oil
1 tablespoon preserved black bean
2 tablespoons Sichuan chilli bean paste (doubanjiang) or sriracha or your favourite chilli sauce
30 g (1 oz) fresh ginger, finely chopped
6 cloves garlic, finely chopped
100 ml (3½ fl oz) water
1 tablespoon light soy sauce
2 teaspoons sugar
2 tablespoons black vinegar
salt to taste
1½ tablespoons cornflour mixed with 3 tablespoons water to make a thickening slurry
small handful of coriander, chopped, to garnish (optional)

For the fish, prepare a steamer with a lid over a wok or a large pot with at least 2 litres (70 fl oz) of boiling water. Rub the rice wine and salt over salmon fillets and lay them on the dish skin-side down. Top with the ginger slices.

Steam the fish for 15-20 minutes until cooked. Use a chopstick to poke through the flesh at the thickest point; if there's resistance, steam for a little longer. Once the fish is cooked, remove the sliced ginger and turn off the steamer but let it sit in the residual heat so the fish stays hot.

For the chilli sauce, place the oil, black bean and chilli bean paste in a wok or medium pan and cook over a high heat, constantly moving it around to prevent burning, until fragrant (about 1 minute). Add the ginger and garlic and fry for another 1 minute. Add in the water plus the cooking liquid from the steamed fillets (hold the fish in place with chopsticks and tilt the juices from the dish into the wok/pan). Add in the soy sauce, sugar and black vinegar. Bring to a simmer for 1 minute and taste. Add salt if required.

Reduce the heat to medium. Slowly stir in as much of the slurry as needed to reach your desired consistency — it should resemble a thick pouring gravy. Turn off the heat.

Pour the sauce over the top of the fish. Garnish with coriander, if desired.

THE LOWDOWN

Season the salmon and steam with ginger. In a pan or wok, fry aromatics, add water and juices from fish with seasoning, thicken the sauce and pour over fish. Approx. 25 minutes.

EASY STEAMED FISH FILLETS

Okay, I get it, I keep saying 'this is my favourite dish' but this one's special for sure. If you have grown up in a Cantonese household like me, this dish will most likely be up there in your top 10 dishes.

Prepare a steamer with a lid over a wok or a large pot with at least 2 litres (70 fl oz) of boiling water. If using a microwave, use a microwave-safe dish deep enough for the fish and liquids that will be produced.

Lay the whole fish fillets on a steaming/microwave dish. If using a large fish like salmon, cut the fish fillets smaller, into 3 cm (1¼ in) thick pieces.

In a bowl mix the remaining ingredients, except the ginger and spring onion. Pour over the fish, rotating it a couple of times to make sure it is covered with the seasoning liquid.

Place the ginger and spring onion whites over the fish and steam over a high heat for 15-20 minutes, depending on the size of the fish. If using the microwave, cover the dish and microwave for 10-12 minutes (depending on strength of your microwave), or until the fish is cooked. Be very careful not to get burned by the steam when you remove the lid. Use a chopstick to poke through the thickest part of the fish to check doneness. If there is resistance, steam/microwave a little longer.

SERVES 2-4 AS A PROTEIN SIDE WITH RICE

- 600g–800 g (1 lb 5 oz–1 lb 12 oz) fresh or frozen fish fillets of your choice (thawed frozen basa works well)
- 1 tablespoon Shaoxing or any aromatic rice wine
- ¼ cup light soy sauce
- 1½ teaspoons salt
- ¼ teaspoon white pepper
- 3 tablespoons sugar
- 2 tablespoons oil
- 1 teaspoon chicken bouillon powder (optional)
- 50 g (1¾ oz) fresh ginger, sliced
- 2 spring onions, greens and whites julienned or diagonally sliced

THE LOWDOWN

Place fish in a dish for steaming or microwaving. Mix the seasoning and pour over fish with aromatics on top, steam or microwave until cooked. Approx. 25 minutes.

STEAMED BLUE COD WITH SIZZLING OIL

The high fat content of the blue cod balanced with sweet soy and aromatics from the exploded oil allows the gingery flavour to come through. Mixed with rice, it becomes a heavenly combo. Whole steamed fish, especially blue cod, is considered a celebratory dish and commonly found in the middle of banquet dinners on special occasions such as New Year and birthdays.

A whole fish is symbolic of 'the entirety' because it has the head and tail still attached, meaning that life will reach full completion, whether in terms of success or love. (At times it's steamed in pairs to really make it obvious . . .)

SERVES 2-4 AS A PROTEIN SIDE WITH RICE

- 1 medium whole blue cod (600–800 g/1 lb 5 oz–1 lb 12 oz), guts cleaned and descaled
- ½ cup light soy sauce
- 3 tablespoons rice wine
- 1½ teaspoons salt
- ¼ teaspoon white pepper
- 3 tablespoons sugar
- 1 teaspoon chicken bouillon powder (optional)
- 100 g (3½ oz) spring onions, greens and whites julienned separately
- 1 tablespoon preserved black bean (optional)
- 1 medium chilli pepper, thinly sliced (optional)
- 50 g (1¾ oz) fresh ginger, julienned
- 80 ml (2¾ fl oz) high-smoke-point oil (peanut or vegetable)

Prepare a large steamer with a lid over a wok or large pot with at least 2 litres (70 fl oz) boiling water.

Make 3 diagonal slices across each side of the fish. Lay the fish on a large dish with at least 3 cm (1¼ in) depth to capture the juices from the fish as it cooks.

In a bowl, mix the soy sauce, rice wine, salt, white pepper, sugar and chicken bouillon together. Pour this seasoning liquid over the fish and rotate the fish a couple of times to make sure it is covered with seasoning liquid.

Sprinkle the spring onion whites, black bean and chilli slices, if using, and half the ginger over the fish and steam over a high heat for 15-20 minutes, depending on the size of the fish. Use a chopstick to poke through the thickest part of the fish to check doneness. If there is resistance going through the fish, steam a little longer.

Once the fish is done, turn off the heat and sprinkle over the spring onion greens and the remaining ginger. In a small pan/pot heat the oil to 220°C (400°F) (almost smoking) and pour over the garnish to make the 'sizzle'.

Substitutions: Any fish with high fat content works well, for example salmon, trout, sole or flounder. Fish fillets work well for smaller portions or if you have smaller steamer baskets.

THE LOWDOWN

Place whole fish in a large dish for steaming. Mix the seasonings and pour over fish with aromatics on top. Steam until cooked. Heat oil in a pan and pour over fish. Approx. 30 minutes.

SQUID WITH CELERY

The contrast of chew and crunch from the squid and celery makes this Cantonese dish really interesting — it's delicate in flavour and incredibly easy to make. If you can find fresh squid, even better, but more often than not I use frozen squid/calamari tubes and they are just as good. This dish brings something unique to the banquet table.

Scoring the squid is totally optional, however, it allows the squid to 'flower up', which is not only visually pleasing but helps the squid carry more flavour from the sauce.

Bring a kettle or a small pot of water to a boil.

If you're using fresh squid, clean it and pull out the innards. Pull the tentacles away from the main tube. Cut below the eyes and discard the innards along with the quill in the main body, beak and eyes. Section the tentacles, if they are longer than 6 cm (2½ in) cut them in half.

For both fresh and defrosted frozen squid, open up the main section of the head and score the inside in 2 mm (1/16 in) scores in a criss-cross pattern. Cut the squid into approx 5 cm x 3 cm (2 in x 1¼ in) sections. Place in a bowl. Pour the boiling water over the squid, moving the pieces about with chopsticks for about 20 seconds. Drain off the water in a colander in the sink. This will precook the squid and remove any impurities. Shake the squid dry and set aside.

Heat a large pan/wok over a medium-high heat, add the oil and garlic and fry for 30 seconds until fragrant. Increase the heat to high and throw in the squid and rice wine. Cook for 30 seconds, moving the squid around. Add the celery and cook for a further 1 minute. Add the remaining ingredients, except the sesame oil. Continue to stir-fry on high for 30 seconds then turn off the heat. Stir in the sesame oil, and plate.

SERVES 2-4 AS A PROTEIN SIDE WITH RICE

500 g (1 lb 2 oz) fresh squid or 400 g (14 oz) thawed frozen squid tubes
1 litre (35 fl oz) boiling water
3 tablespoons oil
5 cloves garlic, thinly sliced
1 teaspoon rice wine
200 g (7 oz) stalks celery, cut into diagonal 3 cm (1¼ in) slices
1 teaspoon salt
1 teaspoon sugar
pinch of white pepper
½ teaspoon cornflour mixed with 1 teaspoon water to make a thickening slurry
1 teaspoon sesame oil

THE LOWDOWN

Pour boiling water over cleaned, prepared and cut squid for 20 seconds. Fry aromatics until fragrant and stir-fry the celery with the squid. Season and thicken with slurry. Approx. 15 minutes.

SALT AND PEPPER SQUID

This Chinese classic became a staple in my diet growing up and for many, this is the gateway into an obsession with squid. The tenderness of perfectly cooked squid in combination with the crisp texture from the fried outer coating and the addictive salty, spicy flavour is truly remarkable.

In a small bowl, combine all the spice mix ingredients and set aside.

If you're using fresh squid, clean it and pull out the innards. Pull the tentacles away from the main tube, cut below the eyes and discard the innards along with the quill in the main body, beak and eyes. Section the tentacles, if they are longer than 6 cm (2½ in) cut them in half (see note page 160). Set the tentacles aside.

For both fresh and defrosted frozen squid, open up the main section of the head and score the inside in 2 mm (1/16 in) scores in a criss-cross pattern (see note page 160). Cut the squid into approx 5 cm x 5 cm (2 in x 2 in) sections. Place in a bowl together with the tentacles. Pat the squid dry with a clean tea towel or paper towel.

Add in the rice wine, egg yolk and salt and mix thoroughly. Add in the regular flour and 2 tablespoons cornflour to create a wet batter to soak the squid.

Preheat the frying oil in a shallow pot or wok to about 190°C (375°F), or when the oil bubbles around a wooden skewer or chopstick when you dip it in.

Place the ½ cup cornflour in a separate bowl. Pick each piece of squid from the batter, coat with the dry cornflour and set aside on a plate.

Fry the squid, in batches if your pot/wok is smaller, for about 2–3 minutes, or until lightly golden.

Store the frying oil for future use but leave about 2 tablespoons in the pan/wok. Bring the oil back up to medium heat and fry the garlic, chilli and spring onion whites for 45 seconds, or until super fragrant. Increase the heat to high, add in the squid and spice mix and stir-fry for 30 seconds.

THE LOWDOWN

Clean and cut the squid into portions. Mix the prepared squid with batter and fry in batches. In a pan/wok fry the aromatics and seasoning and stir through the fried squid. Approx. 20 minutes.

SERVES 2–4 AS A PROTEIN SIDE WITH RICE

Spice mix
¼ teaspoon white pepper
1 teaspoon salt
1 teaspoon sugar
½ teaspoon chicken bouillon powder (optional)
¼ teaspoon ground toasted Sichuan pepper (optional)

400 g (14 oz) whole squid or tubes (fresh or frozen)
1 tablespoon rice wine
1 egg yolk
½ teaspoon salt
1 tablespoon flour
2 tablespoons + ½ cup cornflour
500 ml (17 fl oz) oil for frying
3 cloves garlic, finely diced
1 red chilli, deseeded if desired, and thinly sliced
2 spring onion whites, finely chopped or ¼ small brown onion, finely diced

HONEY WALNUT SHRIMP

This dish is a perfect example of assimilated Chinese food, utilising what ingredients are available in the West to fuse with Chinese cooking techniques to make something new. In my opinion it's a definite crowd-pleaser. It has been popularised by takeaway shops and chains in the US, and though it's rarer here in Aotearoa, you can get it in a handful of Cantonese restaurants. Here is my version.

SERVES 2-4 AS A PROTEIN SIDE WITH RICE

Sauce
- ¾ cup mayonnaise
- 2 tablespoons honey
- 2 tablespoons sweetened condensed milk
- 2 tablespoons freshly squeezed lemon juice

Walnuts
- ¼ cup water
- ⅓ cup brown sugar
- 20 g (¾ oz) butter
- 150 g (5½ oz) walnut halves
- ¼ teaspoon salt

Prawns
- 400 g (14 oz) prawns (fresh or thawed frozen), shelled and tail left on ½ teaspoon salt
- pinch of white pepper
- 2 egg whites
- ¼ cup flour
- 2 tablespoons cornflour
- 500 ml (17 fl oz) oil for frying

For the sauce, mix all the ingredients together in a bowl.

For the walnuts, place the water and sugar in a small pan and bring it to a gentle simmer while stirring (approx. 1 minute). Over a medium heat, add in the butter, walnuts and salt. Stir to coat the walnuts while reducing the sugar until it becomes thick like caramel, approx. 4-6 minutes. Lay the walnuts on baking paper or a plate to cool down and get crunchy. If they're not crunchy, bake in an oven preheated to 150°C (300°F) for a further 10 minutes.

Prepare the prawns by deveining, if desired, and patting them dry with paper towels. Place in a bowl with the salt and pepper and mix thoroughly to coat. Add the egg whites and flours to the bowl to form a batter.

Heat the oil in a shallow pan/wok to about 180°C (350°F), or when the oil bubbles around a wooden skewer or chopstick when you dip it in. Fry the prawns in the oil for about 3-4 minutes, in batches if the pan is small. Once all the prawns are fried once, fry them again for 1 minute — the second time is to get a crispier coating.

Place the prawns in a bowl, pour over the sauce and coat well. Add in the walnuts and stir through.

THE LOWDOWN

Reduce the sugar and walnuts in a small pot, lay them on baking paper and crisp up in the oven, if necessary. Season the prawns, coat with batter, fry then coat with the sauce and walnuts. Approx. 30 minutes.

Modern Chinese

MEAT

CRISPY CANTONESE-STYLE PORK BELLY

Cantonese-style crispy roast pork belly might be the most celebrated dish among my peers. It's an absolute crowd-pleaser and makes for an impressive centre-stage dish. One of my all-time favourite things to cook and eat at home, it's a great make-ahead dish to have for easy meals during the week. I've played around with this recipe and worked out a great way to execute the crispy crackling skin result using a simple home kitchen oven setup and a sharp knife with a pointy tip . . .

Preheat the oven to 220°C (425°F).

Prepping the pork belly is crucial. The belly should be dry. Any excess moisture will prevent it from crisping up nicely. Use paper towels or allow the pork to dry out in the fridge the night before, skin-side up. If the piece of belly you have is thicker on one end or has bones (ribs) attached, trim the belly and/or remove the ribs to even out the belly thickness to ensure an even cook throughout. Keep the trimmed meat/ribs for stir-fries or broths, or freeze them for future use.

Cut slices on the meat side of the belly about 1 cm (½ in) deep and 2–3 cm (1 in) apart (this allows for a deeper marination and reduces the meat curling when cooking).

On the skin side, using the very sharp tip of a small knife/metal skewer poke as many holes as you can, penetrating the skin into the fat. Basically you want the fat seeping to the top to fry the skin when roasting.

Mix all the ingredients for the marinade in a small bowl and rub on the meat side of the belly, making sure to get the marinade into the cuts and trying your best to not get any on the skin. Rub it in and flip the meat over onto some tin foil lined with baking paper. Fold the tin foil around the pork so it covers the sides but the skin is exposed. This will help prevent the sides burning.

Using a paper towel, dry the skin and brush on the oil and vinegar. Sprinkle the salt evenly on top of the skin.

Bake as follows:

First temp: 220°C (425°F) for 20–25 minutes to start heating up the meat for the rendering process of the fat.

Second temp: 170°C (325°F) for 55–60 minutes (or until the

Recipe continued overleaf

SERVES 4–6 AS A PROTEIN SIDE WITH RICE

1–2 kg (2 lb 4 oz–4 lb 8 oz) pork belly (20 per cent-or more fat is ideal)
2 teaspoons neutral oil
1 tablespoon white vinegar
2–3 tablespoons salt

Marinade
2 tablespoons sugar
1 tablespoon chicken bouillon powder
1 teaspoon garlic powder
1 teaspoon onion powder
¼ teaspoon white pepper
2 teaspoons cumin powder
1 teaspoon five-spice powder
1½ tablespoons salt
1 tablespoon cornflour
1½ tablespoons rice wine

meat is tender — poke the sides with a fork, if it pierces with minimal resistance, it's done). This temperature is to slowly cook the pork until tender.

Third temp: 220°C (425°F) for 10-15 minutes, or until the crackling is crispy and deep golden. Allow to rest 10-15 minutes before carving.

To make it easier I usually cut the pork skin-side down on the chopping board to prevent the skin from falling off. Use a heavy meat cleaver/chef's knife.

If the skin is a little burnt, don't panic — it's actually quite common even in professional Hong Kong roast-meat places. Simply scrape the burnt parts off the crackling.

THE LOWDOWN

Dry the pork belly, slice cuts on the meat side and poke holes on the skin side. Mix the marinade and rub onto the meat side. Roast in the oven at 3 different temperatures. Approx. 1.5–2 hours depending on the size of the belly.

RED-BRAISED PORK BELLY

Red-braised is a term used in Chinese cooking for the colour of the protein when prepared, a deep dark red that's glistening, vibrant and extremely drool-worthy to look at. In some Chinese regions, the colour is traditionally created by cooking rock sugar in oil until it turns a dark caramel colour, giving the food that redness. My method is much simpler, using dark soy sauce to achieve a similar effect. Red-braised pork has many different regional variations, mainly in the spices used, but they are all generally sweet, savoury and sticky with the use of rice wine, soy sauce, sugar and ginger.

Cut the pork belly into 4 cm (1½ in) cubes. Depending on the size of the belly, the cube sizes will be different; as long as the cubes are all a similar size it will work.

Heat a large pot/wok over a high heat, add the oil and bring it to almost smoking point. Add in the ginger, garlic and spring onion whites and fry, stirring constantly, for 30 seconds or until aromatic and slightly caramelised. Add the pork belly pieces and continue to cook on high until the pork becomes firm, about 5 minutes. Add in the soy sauces, salt, white pepper, chicken bouillon and bay leaves, star anise and cloves, if using. Continue to fry for a few minutes.

Pour in the rice wine and cook to reduce for a few minutes, stirring constantly. It should be bubbling at this point so the alcohol is being evaporated. Add the water and sugar and bring to a gentle simmer. Reduce the heat to medium-low and cook, covered, for 45-60 minutes until the pork is tender, checking on the pork every 10 minutes or so and giving it a stir.

Remove the lid, add in the spring onion greens and let the liquids reduce for 5-10 minutes. Taste and adjust seasoning if needed.

SERVES 4-6 AS A PROTEIN SIDE WITH RICE

- 1–1.5 kg (2 lb 4 oz–3 lb 5 oz) pork belly with skin on (ideally 20–30 per cent fat)
- 3 tablespoons oil
- 50 g (1¾ oz) fresh ginger, sliced
- 8 cloves garlic, smacked
- 3 spring onions, whites and greens cut separately into 3 cm (1¼ in) pieces
- ½ cup light soy sauce
- 3 tablespoons dark soy sauce
- 2 tablespoons salt
- ½ teaspoon white pepper
- 1 tablespoon chicken bouillon powder
- 4-5 bay leaves (optional)
- 4 star anise (optional)
- 8 cloves (optional)
- 1 cup rice wine
- 200 ml (7 fl oz) water
- ½ cup sugar

THE LOWDOWN

Fry aromatics with pork, add water, seasonings and simmer. Add garnishes and reduce sauce. Approx. 90 minutes.

TWICE-COOKED PORK WITH CUMIN

The precooking of the pork belly here means the second cook of the pork is purely to caramelise and render the fat, which seasons the vegetables that are tossed with spices. It's the perfect dish for maximum rice-eating potential. I highly recommend cooking more pork than you need and freezing the sliced portions for future use or keep in the fridge to be cooked in the next few days.

In a medium-sized pot large enough to fit the whole pork belly and water, add in all the ingredients for the pork preparation and bring to a simmer. Allow the pork to simmer on medium-low for 25 minutes, or until the pork is cooked and slightly tender. Turn off the heat and discard the water. Cool the pork belly completely in the fridge, for 1 hour minimum or ideally overnight.

Once the pork belly is completely cooled, cut into slices about 4-5 mm (¼ in) thick.

Heat the oil in a large pan/wok and fry the pork belly slices over a high heat until the pork is developing some colour and rendering the fat out, about 5 minutes. Add the garlic, dark soy sauce, cumin seeds, chilli flakes and black bean, if using. Fry until aromatic, about 3 minutes.

Add the leek, capsicum, salt, sugar and ground cumin and continue to stir-fry for about 3-4 minutes until the leek is cooked and translucent.

Turn off the heat, stir through the chopped fresh chilli, if using, and taste and adjust seasoning if needed.

SERVES 2-4 AS A PROTEIN SIDE WITH RICE

Pork preparation

300 g (10½ oz) boneless skin-on pork belly (ideally 20–30 per cent fat)
1 litre (35 fl oz) water
30 g (1 oz) fresh ginger, sliced
2 tablespoons salt

Second cook

2 tablespoons oil
3 cloves garlic, minced
1 teaspoon dark soy sauce
1 teaspoon cumin seeds
1 tablespoon chilli flakes
1 tablespoon fermented black bean (optional but highly recommended)
100 g (3½ oz) leek or ½ a small leek, cut into 3 cm (1¼ in) slices
½ capsicum, deseeded and cut into 2 cm (¾ in) slices
1 teaspoon salt
2 teaspoons sugar
1 teaspoon ground cumin
1 small red fresh chilli, chopped (optional)

THE LOWDOWN

Boil the pork belly until cooked and cool. Fry sliced, cooled pork belly with aromatics, seasoning and vegetables. 30 minutes to cook pork, 10 minutes to stir-fry after overnight cooling of pork.

SIMPLE CUMIN AND CHILLI LAMB SKEWERS

I discovered the wonderful flavours of northern Chinese cuisine only about five years ago in some of the increasingly popular regional Chinese food establishments along Dominion Road in Auckland. Since then I've developed an affinity for these explosive flavours. Think charred meats with the combination of pungent cumin and chilli, or noodles submerged in meat broths glowing with red chilli oil.

This dish is something I crave often and is commonly found in northern Chinese regional eateries. It is best shared with friends and makes the perfect drinking food/snack.

Have enough bamboo or metal skewers (20-25 cm/8-10 in) for this recipe.

Prepare the lamb by trimming off some of the fat if the piece you have is too fatty. About 10 per cent fat is a good amount to keep on the meat as the fat will help season the meat and prevent it from drying out. Cut the meat into 1.5-2 cm (¾ in) chunks and place into a bowl.

Season the lamb with the remaining ingredients, mix well and allow to marinate for at least 2 hours or overnight in the fridge.

Soak bamboo skewers in warm water for an hour before using.

Skewer the lamb chunks, with approx. 6-8 pieces of lamb on each skewer.

Preheat a barbecue grill or grill pan to maximum heat. Grill the skewers, about 3-5 minutes on each side.

If you are dusting extra seasoning on top, mix the cumin, chilli powder and salt in a small bowl and sprinkle pinches of the spice mix over the skewers with each turn during the cook. You should have charred bits on the lamb and crispy bits on the edges.

MAKES 12-18 SKEWERS

600–800 g (1 lb 5 oz–1 lb 12 oz) lamb shoulder meat (with fat)
1½ tablespoons salt
¼ teaspoon white pepper
2 teaspoons garlic powder
2 teaspoons onion powder
2 tablespoons ground cumin
3 tablespoons chilli flakes

For dusting (optional)
1 tablespoon ground cumin
1 teaspoon chilli powder
1 teaspoon salt

THE LOWDOWN

Cut the lamb into small chunks and marinate with seasoning. Skewer the meat and grill over charcoal or in a pan, then dust with extra seasoning. Approx. 30 minutes plus marination time.

XL CUMIN AND CHILLI LAMB SKEWERS

This version of lamb skewers is for people who appreciate the rich flavours of lamb meat and fat intertwined. It's the perfect recipe for when you have a hunk of lamb with a good amount of fat attached. The smoky, charred meat laced with pungent spices make this one of the most enticing dishes from northern China.

MAKES 10-12 SKEWERS

Spice mix
2 tablespoons coriander seeds
2 tablespoons cumin seeds
1 teaspoon white peppercorns
1 teaspoon Sichuan peppercorns
1 tablespoon salt
1 tablespoon sugar
1 teaspoon garlic powder
1 tablespoon ground cumin
3 tablespoons chilli flakes
½ teaspoon chilli powder (optional)

600–800 g (1 lb 5 oz–1 lb 12 oz) lamb shoulder meat (with high fat)
1 medium brown onion
1½ tablespoons salt
1 teaspoon cracked black pepper
¼ teaspoon white pepper
1 teaspoon garlic powder
½ cup rice wine

For the spice mix, toast the seeds and peppercorns in a dry pan over a medium heat until aromatic (approx. 5 minutes). In a mortar and pestle or spice grinder, add these along with the salt, sugar, garlic powder, ground cumin, chilli flakes and optional chilli powder for extra kick. Grind to form a fine powder. Set aside.

Trim off any large area of surface fat from the meat, cut into chunks and reserve. Cut the lamb meat into approx. 2-3 cm (1 in) cubes. Blanch the chunks of lamb fat in 1 litre (35 fl oz) of boiling water over a high heat until solid (approx. 5 minutes). Take out the fat, shake off excess water, allow to cool slightly and cut into 2 cm (¾ in) cubes.

Peel and cut the onion into large chunks. It is used to impart flavour into the meat only.

In a bowl marinate the lamb, lamb fat, onion chunks, salt, black pepper, white pepper, garlic powder and rice wine for at least 2 hours or overnight in the fridge.

Soak bamboo skewers in warm water for an hour if using.

Skewer alternating pieces of meat and fat. There should be 4 or 5 pieces of meat on each skewer. Discard the onions.

Preheat a barbecue or grill pan to maximum heat. Grill the skewers for about 2-3 minutes on each of the 4 sides of the cube. Sprinkle a generous amount of the spice mix over the skewers with each turn during the cook. You should have charred bits on the lamb and the fat pieces will be rendered and crispy on the edges.

THE LOWDOWN
Cut and separate the fat and meat of the lamb. Poach the fat and cut into cubes along with the meat, season and marinate. Toast spices and grind. Skewer the meat and grill over charcoal or in a pan, dust with extra seasoning. Approx. 40 minutes plus marination time.

SPICY BLACK BEAN BEEF

Growing up in and around my parents' Chinese takeaway shop, black bean beef stir-fries have always been a constant on the menu.

For me a great black bean beef is made with tender, juicy beef, minimal vegetables and a touch of chilli amping it to another level. Here's my rendition of this takeaway classic.

Thinly slice the beef into 3 mm thick (⅛ in) strips about 4 cm (1½ in) long and place into a bowl. Add in all the marinade ingredients, mix through the beef well and let sit for at least 15 minutes to infuse. The baking soda helps break down the meat protein, allowing it to get even more tender.

Heat 3 tablespoons oil in a wok/large pan over a high heat and stir-fry the beef, separating the strips until they are almost cooked through, about 3-4 minutes. Remove from the wok and set aside.

In the same wok/pan add the 1 tablespoon oil, black bean, chilli, ginger and garlic, and stir-fry over a high heat for 30 seconds until aromatic. Add the capsicum and fry for a further 1 minute. Add the beef back in and fry for a further 30 seconds. Turn off the heat and serve.

THE LOWDOWN

Marinate the beef for at least 15 minutes. Fry the beef and set aside. Fry aromatics and vegetables then return the beef. Approx. 30 minutes including marination time.

SERVES 2-4 AS A PROTEIN SIDE WITH RICE

350 g (12 oz) beef steak (sirloin, scotch or eye fillet)
3 tablespoons + 1 tablespoon oil
2 tablespoons fermented black bean
1 tablespoon chilli flakes or 1-2 small fresh red chillis, finely chopped
10 g (¼ oz) fresh ginger, finely chopped
3 cloves garlic, finely chopped
1 capsicum, deseeded and cut into 2 cm (¾ in) pieces

Marinade
1 tablespoon rice wine
2 teaspoons salt
1 teaspoon light soy sauce
1 teaspoon dark soy sauce
1 teaspoon sugar
1 tablespoon cornflour
½ teaspoon baking soda (optional)
2 tablespoons water

BRAISED BEEF BRISKET WITH DAIKON

Braised beef with daikon (Asian radish) is a classic Chinese dish that's great for serving a large group.

There's a little preparation before the slow braising, but the rewards are incredibly high: falling-apart beef brisket with soft braised daikon that has soaked up all the savoury sauce — a magical combination. This is optional but if you can find fresh beef tendon at the Asian grocer butchery section, add some to this dish during the braise for extra gelatinous richness. Apparently it's great for collagen rejuvenation for the skin . . . well, that's what the Asian aunties tell me, anyway.

SERVES 6-8 AS A PROTEIN SIDE WITH RICE

- 1 kg (2 lb 4 oz) beef brisket (with fat on), cut into 4 cm (1½ in) cubes
- 3 tablespoons + 1 tablespoon oil
- 30 g (1 oz) fresh ginger, sliced
- 8 cloves garlic, smacked
- 2 spring onions, cut into 4 cm (1½ in) segments
- 500 g (1 lb 2 oz) beef tendon, cut into 3 cm (1¼ in) chunks (optional)
- 1 teaspoon black peppercorn
- 4 bay leaves (fresh or dried)
- 1 teaspoon five-spice powder
- 5 g (1/8 oz) dried tangerine/citrus peel (optional)
- 1 litre (35 fl oz) stock or water
- 800 g (1 lb 12 oz) daikon (1 medium size), peeled and cut into 4 cm (1½ in) cubes

Ingredients continued on opposite page

This part is optional but highly recommended for extra depth of flavour. In a heated large fry pan/wok or pot, add 3 tablespoons oil and brown the beef brisket over a high heat. Sear each side of the beef cubes by turning them as they caramelise (approx 1 minute on each side). If your pan is small, do it in batches and set aside.

If you don't feel like searing the beef brisket, in a mixing bowl with the cut beef chunks, pour a whole kettle (approx 1.5 litres/52 fl oz) of boiling water over the meat and agitate with tongs. Pour out the water and pat the beef dry.

In a large pot/wok or pressure cooker add 1 tablespoon oil and fry the ginger, garlic and spring onion over a high heat for about 1 minute until aromatic. Add in all the rest of the ingredients, except the daikon, including the seasoning, beef tendons, and the seared or rinsed beef brisket. If using a pot or wok, bring everything to a gentle simmer over a medium heat with the lid on and braise for 60-80 minutes (40-50 minutes in a pressure cooker).

At this stage add in the daikon and braise for another 40 minutes (lid on), or until the beef is tender and the daikon is soft when pierced. If using a pressure cooker, release the steam and carefully open the pot to add the daikon and pressure cook again for 30 minutes, or until the beef is tender.

Once the meat is tender, skim off most of the fat from the surface of the broth and taste. Adjust the seasoning if needed. If you want the sauce thick like gravy, pour in the thickening slurry and bring it back to a simmer.

Seasoning

½ cup rice wine
¼ cup light soy sauce
¼ cup oyster sauce
1 tablespoon salt
2 tablespoons sugar
⅓ teaspoon white pepper
2 tablespoons hoisin sauce (optional)
3 red fermented beancurd cubes (optional)
2 tablespoons cornflour mixed with 2 tablespoons water to make a thickening slurry (optional)

THE LOWDOWN

Sear or hot-water rinse the beef chunks. Fry the aromatics in a pot/wok/pressure cooker with the beef. Add seasoning and liquids to braise for about an hour. Add daikon and braise for another 30 minutes. Approx. 2 hours.

SPICY KUNG PAO CHICKEN

Originally a Sichuan dish, this has gained massive popularity in recent years in the West. Super flavourful, spicy and fragrant with toasted chilli and crunchy peanuts, it's a flavour explosion that's surprisingly easy to put together. This is a great dish to raise eyebrows at the dinner table or at a potluck, especially if paired with beer.

SERVES 2-4 AS A PROTEIN SIDE WITH RICE

- 600 g (1 lb 5 oz) boneless chicken thigh fillets, cut into 2–3 cm (1 in) pieces (skin on optional)
- 1½ tablespoons light soy sauce
- 1 teaspoon dark soy sauce
- 1 teaspoon salt
- 2 teaspoons sugar
- 1 teaspoon chicken bouillon powder (optional)
- 1 teaspoon sesame oil
- 1 tablespoon rice wine
- 2 teaspoons cornflour

To cook

- 3 tablespoons oil
- 3 cloves garlic, minced
- 8 dried whole chillis, cut into 2 cm (¾ in) chunks and deseeded if desired, or 2 tablespoons chilli flakes
- ½ small brown onion, cut into 1 cm (½ in) pieces
- ½ cup roasted peanuts
- 1 tablespoon black vinegar
- pinch of ground Sichuan pepper powder (optional)

Place the chicken and all the marinade ingredients in a bowl, and leave for 30-60 minutes.

In a heated wok/large pan over a high heat, add the oil and fry the chicken, trying not to move the pieces around too much so they can caramelise on one side before flipping and moving them. You're aiming to caramelise most sides of the chicken and this will take about 10 minutes, until the chicken is cooked through. Remove the chicken from the pan and set aside.

Using the same wok/pan, add the garlic, chilli and brown onion and stir-fry for 1-2 minutes over a medium heat, or until fragrant and the onion is slightly transparent. Add 1 tablespoon extra oil if the pan/wok is too dry. Turn the heat to high, add the chicken back in with the rest of the ingredients, stir-fry for 1 minute and serve.

THE LOWDOWN

Marinate chicken pieces for approx. 1 hour. Fry the chicken and set aside. Fry the aromatics with the chicken, peanuts and chilli. Approx. 20 minutes to cook plus 30–60 minutes to marinate the chicken.

CLASSIC CHINESE POACHED CHICKEN

This has to be one of the purest ways to cook and eat chicken, literally poaching it in water and then pairing it with a simple soy-based sauce or relish.

With such a simple dish, so much depends on the natural flavour of the chicken so it is important to use a high-quality chicken. In many Chinese households the preference is to use yellow free-range cornfed chickens, as they tend to have a more pure poultry flavour and are slightly sweeter.

SERVES 4–6 AS A PROTEIN SIDE WITH RICE

- 50 g (1¾ oz) fresh ginger, sliced
- 2 spring onions, cut into thirds
- 5 cloves garlic, smacked
- 2 tablespoons salt
- ½ teaspoon ground white pepper
- 2 litres (70 fl oz) water
- 1 whole good-quality chicken (1.6–1.8 kg/3 lb 8 oz–4 lb) or 4 chicken legs or Marylands
- 1 tablespoon sesame oil, to garnish

Place all the ingredients, except the chicken and sesame oil, in a large pot and bring to a boil. Slowly submerge the chicken into the water and move it around so the water temperature evens out in the pot, or pull the chicken out and submerge it again.

Bring the water back to a boil over a medium-high heat. When the water starts to bubble, immediately turn the heat down to the lowest setting and simmer for 20–30 minutes (depending on the size of the chicken) without a lid. Turn off the heat and cover the pot with a lid. Let the chicken sit in the water for at least 20 minutes to cook through. Check the doneness of the chicken by poking the thickest part with a chopstick and if the juices run clear the meat is cooked. Take it out of the water to cool slightly for chopping. Brush the sesame oil on the skin — for aroma and to make the chicken more visually appealing.

Using a cleaver, chop the chicken, bones and all, into bite-sized pieces that can be picked up with chopsticks, or you can pick the meat off the chicken and serve on a plate.

Reserve the stock for future use — it's great for blanching vegetables, or used instead of water for some dishes. The stock is handy to have in the freezer also.

Serve with at least one of these condiments:

Chilli Soy Sauce
In a bowl, mix ⅓ cup light soy sauce, 3 sliced fresh chillis, 1 teaspoon sesame oil and 2 teaspoons sugar. Microwave for 30 seconds to dissolve the sugar.

Exploding Ginger and Spring Onion Relish (see page 196)
Sweet Fragrant Soy Sauce (see page 202)

THE LOWDOWN

Add chicken to a pot of water with aromatics and simmer slowly. Chop and serve with relish or soy-based sauce. Approx. 1 hour.

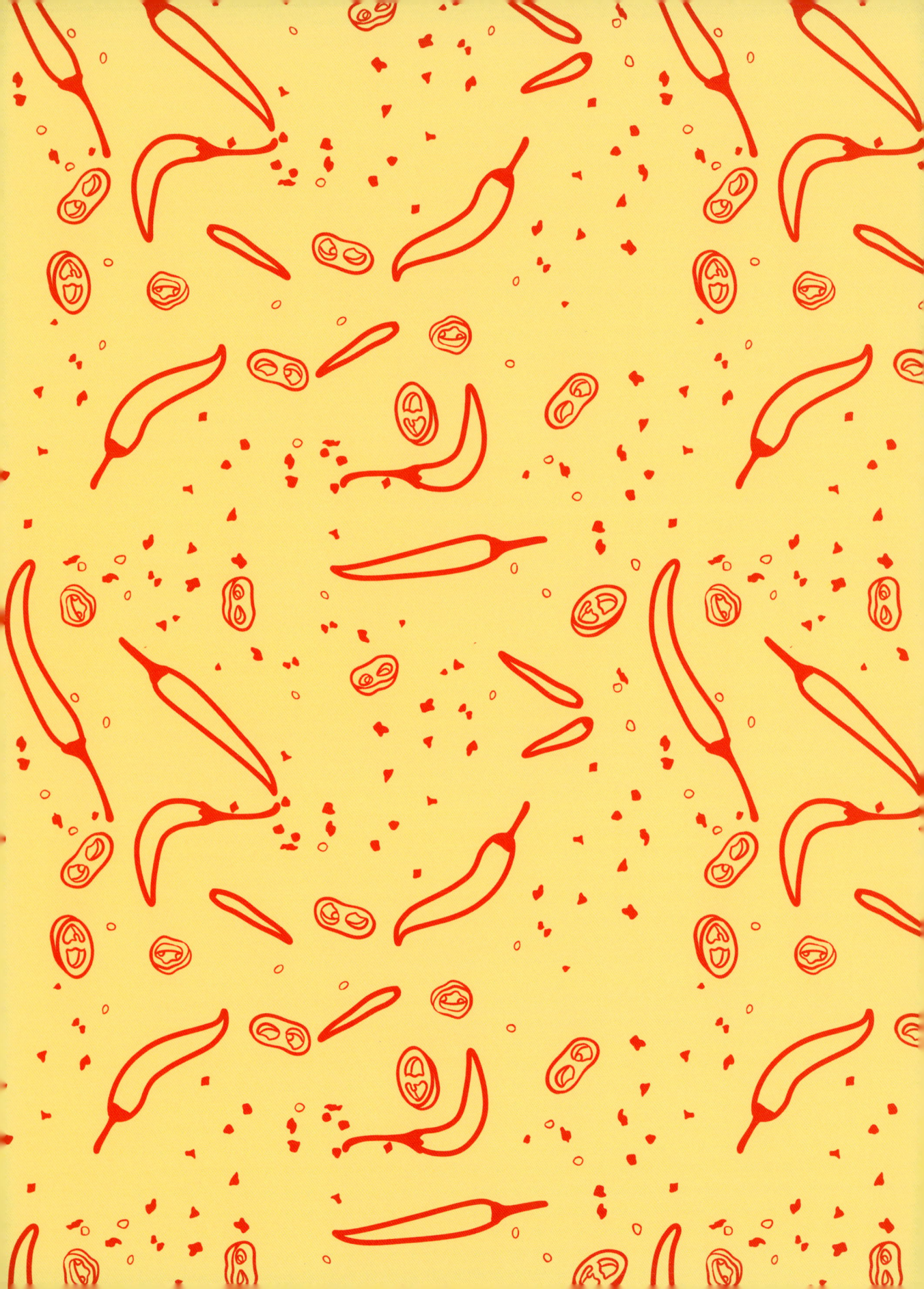

SAUCES & DRESSINGS

BASIC RED CHILLI OIL

In the last 10 years, I have noticed how Chinese-style chilli oils have become a staple in many households' pantries. This is thanks to the rise in international students from China, more specifically central China, travelling abroad to study or start new lives. Because central Chinese flavours are so unique, and a large part of the cuisine is centered around the use of chillis and aromatic oils, Asian grocers around the globe have seen increased demand to import and stock chilli oils for people missing those flavours from their hometown. They eventually made their way into the Western pantry and now we all get to enjoy the aromatic and wonderfully spicy complexity.

Here are a few easy chilli oils you can make at home to have as a pantry staple to really amp up your meals. Decanted into a pretty jar, they also make incredible gifts for loved ones.

In central Chinese cooking this red oil is often used as a finishing oil, doused over or mixed into a stir-fry when the dish is cooked. It adds a lovely toasty roasted chilli aroma and slight heat to any dish.

In a small pot, heat the oil to 160-170°C (315-325°F).

Place the chilli flakes in a heatproof bowl (a thick glass bowl works well).

Pour the hot oil over the chilli and give it a gentle stir — the oil should make the chilli sizzle, slightly darken in colour and give off a rich, roasty aroma. Sprinkle in the sesame seeds, if using.

Allow the chilli oil to cool completely before transferring into airtight jars. Always use a clean utensil when handling to prevent spoilage. It can last for up to 3 months in the pantry.

MAKES APPROX. 400 ML (14 FL OZ)

350 ml (12 fl oz) cooking oil (canola, vegetable or peanut)
100 g (3½ oz) dried ground chilli flakes
1 tablespoon sesame seeds (optional)

THE LOWDOWN

Heat the oil in a pot. Pour over the chilli flakes in a heatproof bowl. Approx. 10 minutes.

AROMATIC CHILLI OIL

If you have never tried making your own aromatic chilli oil or chilli crisp (a chilli condiment in oil, loved for its crunchy bits), this is the recipe that will get you addicted to creating your own. Friends have told me that they would never go back to store-bought chilli oils after making this version. Oh, and did I mention it's incredibly easy?

MAKES APPROX. 500 ML (17 FL OZ)

- 500 ml (17 fl oz) cooking oil (canola, vegetable or peanut)
- 8 cloves garlic, smacked
- 50 g (1¾ oz) fresh ginger, thinly sliced
- 1 small brown onion, peeled and quartered
- 10 g (¼ oz) Sichuan peppercorns
- 6 star anise
- 2 cinnamon sticks
- 4 bay leaves
- 100 g (3½ oz) ground chilli flakes
- 1 teaspoon chilli powder
- 2 tablespoons salt
- 1 tablespoon sesame seeds (optional)

In a small pot, mix the cold oil, garlic, ginger and onion. Over a medium heat, bring the oil up to 170°C (325°F) to fry the aromatics until dark brown — this will take about 10 minutes. Add in the Sichuan peppercorns, star anise, cinnamon and bay leaves. Leave for 2 minutes to allow the flavours to infuse into the oil. Turn off the heat.

Place the chilli flakes in a heatproof bowl (a thick glass bowl works well). Carefully pour the hot oil through a strainer onto the chilli flakes. Stir to evenly distribute the heat of the oil. It should sizzle and darken the chilli flakes slightly. Stir in the chilli powder, salt and sesame seeds, if using.

Allow the chilli oil to cool completely before transferring into airtight jars. Always use a clean utensil when handling to prevent spoilage. It can last up to 3 months in the pantry.

THE LOWDOWN

Fry the aromatics in the oil until browned. Add the spices. Strain the oil over the chilli flakes in a heatproof bowl. Add other ingredients. Approx. 15 minutes.

THE ULTIMATE CHILLI CRISP OIL

I know! Using the word 'ultimate' is pretty bold and a touch egotistical but trust me, this version has so many aromatic components the complexity and flavour are wonderful. Because of its layered aromas, adding this condiment to simple or basic dishes like blanched veges, stir-fries or fried rice means you don't need many actual ingredients in those dishes! A bottle of this as a gift is truly an exchange of love.

In a pot, mix the cold oil, garlic, ginger and onion. Over a medium heat bring the oil up to 170°C (325°F) to fry the aromatics until dark brown — this will take about 20 minutes. Add in the Sichuan peppercorns, cinnamon, star anise and bay leaves. Leave for 2 minutes to allow the flavours to infuse into the oil. Turn off the heat.

Mix the chilli flakes and fried shallots in a heatproof bowl (a thick glass bowl works well) and carefully pour the hot oil through a strainer onto the combination. Stir to evenly distribute the heat of the oil. It should sizzle and darken the chilli flakes slightly. Stir in the roasted peanuts, chilli powder, sugar, salt and sesame seeds, if using.

Allow the chilli oil to cool completely before transferring into airtight jars. Always use a clean utensil when handling to prevent spoilage. It can last up to 3 months in the pantry.

**MAKES APPROX.
1 LITRE (35 FL OZ)**

- 800 ml (28 fl oz) cooking oil (canola, vegetable or peanut)
- 8 cloves garlic, smacked
- 50 g (1¾ oz) fresh ginger, thickly sliced
- 1 small brown onion, peeled and cut into quarters
- 5 g (⅛ oz) Sichuan peppercorns
- 2 cinnamon sticks
- 6 star anise
- 4 bay leaves
- 100 g (3½ oz) chilli flakes
- 100 g (3½ oz) fried shallots
- 50 g (1¾ oz) roasted peanuts
- 1–2 teaspoons chilli powder
- 2 tablespoons sugar
- 3 tablespoons salt
- 1 tablespoon sesame seeds

THE LOWDOWN

Fry the aromatics in the oil until browned. Add the spices. Strain the oil over the chilli flakes and shallots in a heatproof bowl. Add other ingredients. Approx. 25 minutes.

EXPLODING GINGER AND SPRING ONION RELISH

This flavour bomb is one of my go-to relishes to use with simply cooked white meats such as poached chicken and steamed or pan-fried fish. The ginger and spring onion is kissed with hot oil and will coat your palate, making everything incredibly moreish. The best part: it's super easy to make and will last in the fridge for a few days.

MAKES APPROX. 200 ML (7 FL OZ)

- 50 g (1¾ oz) fresh ginger peeled (if desired) and very finely diced
- 2 spring onions, greens and whites, very finely chopped
- 1½ teaspoons salt
- ½ teaspoon caster sugar
- ¼ teaspoon white pepper
- ⅔ cup oil

Place all the ingredients except the oil in a heatproof bowl and mix to combine.

Heat the oil in a small saucepan until it reaches about 200°C (400°F) — if you put a wooden chopstick in the oil it will create bubbles. Pour the hot oil over the ingredients, being careful as it might splatter.

This is best used after 30 minutes of infusion, and can be made in advance.

THE LOWDOWN

In a heatproof bowl, mix all the ingredients except the oil. Pour the heated oil over to sizzle. Approx. 10 minutes plus 30 minutes' infusing.

STRANGE FLAVOUR SAUCE

The name 'strange flavour' is derived from the direct translation from this sauce's Mandarin Chinese name — and in fact it's not strange at all. It does have an unusually deep, complex flavour that is created through combining a nutty component, commonly Chinese dark-roasted sesame paste, with soy, vinegar and spices.

This sauce is one of the key flavours from the Sichuan region and is great over many dishes including blanched vegetables, poached chicken, fish or noodles.

Pro tip: make this well in advance of your meal so it's ready to be used — it can be stored for up to a week in the fridge. I like to make a big batch of this sauce if I know I'm using it for multiple meals.

In a bowl, mix all the ingredients until well combined. If it's too thick add 1-2 tablespoons hot water to loosen the sauce. Adjust seasoning if needed.

**MAKES APPROX.
180 ML (5¾ FL OZ)**

- 3 tablespoons light soy sauce
- 2 tablespoons Chinese sesame paste (or tahini, or any nut butter)
- 2 teaspoons black vinegar (rice vinegar or white vinegar also work well)
- 2 teaspoons sugar
- 1 teaspoon salt
- 2 teaspoons ground chilli flakes (or 2 tablespoons chilli oil with sediment)
- 2 cloves garlic, minced
- 2 teaspoons sesame oil
- ¼ teaspoon ground Sichuan peppercorns or Sichuan pepper oil (optional)

THE LOWDOWN
Mix everything together. Approx. 5 minutes.

SWEET FRAGRANT SOY SAUCE

Once you make this sweet, complex and incredibly aromatic soy sauce, you'll literally put it on everything and the world will seem so much tastier . . . It's a good time — guaranteed.

My humble advice is to make a big batch of this and store it in squeezy bottles. It makes life in the kitchen so easy — squeeze it on stir-fries, dumplings, wontons, poached chicken . . . or even straight up on steamed rice.

In a small pot, add all the ingredients except the sugar and bring to a really gentle simmer over a low heat for 20 minutes. Turn off the heat and stir in the sugar until dissolved.

Strain the sauce through a sieve and bottle when cooled. Can be stored for up to a couple of months in the fridge.

MAKES APPROX. 300 ML (10½ FL OZ)

- 300 ml (10½ fl oz) light soy sauce
- 20 g (¾ oz) fresh ginger, smacked
- 3 cloves garlic, smacked
- 1 teaspoon fennel seeds
- 1 cinnamon stick or piece of cassia bark
- 1 star anise
- 2 bay leaves
- ½ teaspoon Sichuan peppercorns
- 1 black cardamom (tsaoko nut), cracked open with the side of the knife or smacked with a rolling pin (optional)
- 100 ml (3½ fl oz) water
- 120 g (4¼ oz) sugar

THE LOWDOWN

To a pot of soy sauce, add spices and aromatics and simmer. Add sugar, strain and cool. Approx. 25 minutes.

ASIAN-STYLE ROLL CAKE

Light, fluffy and fun — what's not to love about this dessert?

I'm usually not a huge sweet tooth, so my perfect dessert is light, not too sweet and clean on the palate. These Asian-style cakes are exactly that, and with the option to add your favourite fresh fruit it almost seems guilt-free, even though it's cake.

SERVES 10-12

Cake
1 tablespoon cornflour
1 teaspoon baking powder
¼ cup high-grade flour
2 whole eggs + 3 egg yolks
⅓ cup caster sugar
25 g (1 oz) butter, melted

Cream filling
150 ml (5 fl oz) fresh double cream (40–44 per cent fat) or regular fresh cream
150 ml (5 fl oz) fresh pouring cream (33–37 per cent fat)
40 g (1½ oz) icing sugar
favourite ripe fruits, cleaned and sliced or cut (optional)

Preheat the oven to 170°C (325°F). Line a 28 cm x 33 cm (11 in x 13 in) or similar baking dish with baking paper.

Sift the cornflour, baking powder and flour together into a small bowl.

In a medium-large heatproof bowl, whisk the whole eggs, egg yolks and sugar together until combined. Place the bowl over a double boiler to heat the mix to 45-50°C (113-122°F). Whisk the mixture the whole time to avoid scrambling the eggs. This process will take 5-7 minutes.

Remove from the heat and use an electric whisk to beat the eggs until super fluffy, thickened and pale in colour (approx. 5 minutes). Gently fold in half the flour mix until combined. Fold in the rest of the flour. Pour in the melted butter and fold. Do not overmix.

Pour the mixture into the prepared dish and spread evenly. Bang the dish on the bench to remove bubbles. Bake for 11 minutes. Lift baking paper and sponge out of the dish and cool upside down on another piece of baking paper.

Meanwhile, for the cream filling, combine both creams in a bowl and whisk until the cream is almost at soft peak stage. Sift in the icing sugar and continue whisking the cream until soft peaks form. I find it helpful to have the creams super cold.

To assemble, spread the whipped cream on the lighter-coloured side of the cake, making sure there's more of the cream in the centre and less on the edges. If using, lay the fruit in the centre where most of the cream is. Using the baking paper, roll and tighten the roll (similar to rolling sushi).

Refrigerate for 2 hours or overnight. Slice into 4 cm (1.5 in) thick slices for serving.

THE LOWDOWN

Preheat oven. Whip eggs with sugar over heat until thickened. Fold in flours and butter. Bake in a lined dish and cool. Whip creams with sugar. Place cream and fruit in cake and roll. Wrap and refrigerate. Approx. 40 minutes with overnight cooling.

CHINESE BROWN SUGAR STEAMED CAKE

Steamed cake sounds more difficult than it actually is! These cakes are surprisingly simple to make, delicious and incredibly nostalgic for people who grew up going to yum cha often. Because of the cooking technique they stay moist and soft, a perfect accompaniment for a hot cup of Chinese tea. Here's my easy take on the traditional recipe!

SERVES 6-8

- 4 eggs
- 1 cup muscovado sugar (or ¾ cup brown sugar)
- 1 teaspoon salt
- ½ teaspoon vanilla essence
- 3½ teaspoons baking powder
- ½ cup milk
- ⅓ cup oil
- 50 g (1¾ oz) coconut milk powder or milk powder (optional)
- 1 cup flour

In a medium-sized bowl, whisk the eggs, sugar, salt and vanilla until very well combined (2-3 minutes). Add in the remaining ingredients, except the flour, and whisk for another 2 minutes. Gently stir in the flour, trying to not overmix, for about 1 minute.

Let the batter sit for at least 30 minutes at room temperature to allow the baking powder to react, which will allow the cake to get fluffy during the steaming process.

Prepare a pot for the steamer basket with at least 2 litres (70 fl oz) of water over a medium-high heat.

Line the base of a cake tin or ceramic bowl with baking paper. I use an 18 cm (7 in) springform cake tin for this recipe, and grease the sides with butter and dust with flour to prevent sticking (or you could use a gentle spray of cooking oil).

Cover and steam for 30 minutes on medium-high (depending on your cooking dish this could take longer). Check the doneness by poking a skewer or chopstick through the middle. If it comes out clean the cake is done.

Serve warm with your favourite cup of tea.

THE LOWDOWN

Whisk egg and seasonings together. Add flours and whisk. Let the batter sit. Prepare a steamer and steam batter in a lined cake tin. Serve warm. Approx. 1 hour.

GOOEY CHOCOLATE AND MOCHI BROWNIE

Chocolate brownies: gooey, fudgy and delicious. Why not amp the gooey factor up even more by adding a layer of mochi in the middle? This layer of chewy glutinous rice-flour dough means extra textural pleasure. This recipe is incredibly easy to make and will surely impress.

Preheat the oven to 180°C (350°F). Line a slightly deep baking tray or cake tin with baking paper (approx 20 cm [8 in]) square or round.

For the mochi, mix the ingredients, except the cornflour, in a microwave-safe bowl until well incorporated. Loosely cover the bowl with cling film or a microwavable lid and microwave for 90 seconds. Carefully take the bowl out and remove the cover. Using chopsticks, mix the cooked mochi mixture clockwise in the bowl for about 3-4 minutes — working the dough like this is what creates the chewy texture.

Dust cornflour on a clean surface or chopping board, place the mochi dough on it and dust the cornflour over the dough as well. While the dough is still warm, flatten it out with your fingers by pressing it flat until it reaches the size of your baking dish (it will be placed in between the brownie batter layers). Set aside.

For the brownie, place the chocolate, butter, sugar and salt in a small saucepan over medium-low heat and heat the mixture, stirring, until the chocolate and butter has melted. Transfer the mixture into a mixing bowl and whisk in the eggs until well mixed. Sift in the flour, cocoa powder and baking powder and fold the mixture together until well incorporated.

Pour half the brownie batter into your lined baking tray and spread it to the edges. Lay the flattened mochi dough on top of the batter and pour over the remaining brownie batter, again spreading it to the edges.

Bake for 22-25 minutes. The middle should be wobbly and seem a little underdone; the residual heat will slowly cook the middle and leave it gooey and fudgy. Allow to cool to room temperature before slicing.

SERVES 10-12

Mochi
100 g (3½ oz) glutinous rice flour (cannot be substituted with rice flour)
180 ml (5¾ fl oz) water
2 teaspoons sugar
1 tablespoon cornflour for dusting

Brownie batter
200 g (7 oz) dark chocolate, buttons or chopped (I like it with a minimum of 60 per cent cocoa solids)
200 g (7 oz) unsalted butter
150 g (5½ oz) caster or brown sugar
¼ teaspoon salt
4 eggs
60 g (2¼ oz) flour
80 g (2¾ oz) cocoa powder
1 teaspoon baking powder

THE LOWDOWN

Microwave mochi ingredients and mix. Heat and mix brownie ingredients. Combine brownie ingredients and flattened mochi dough in a dish. Bake. Approx. 1 hour.

EASY COCONUT SAGO

This super-simple dessert is a great way to finish a meal. It's slightly sweet, aromatically coconutty and refreshing with its fresh-fruit components. I grew up eating this dessert at Chinese buffets and large house gatherings. Kids were the main demographic — though in saying that, I fully believe parents make it for their kids because they want some too.

Sago is a pure starch that is extracted from a tropical palm and shaped into small balls. Sago is easily found in both Western and Asian grocers.

SERVES 4

2 litres (70 fl oz) water
½ cup sago
250 g (9 oz) coconut cream
⅓ cup pure maple syrup or ¼ cup sugar
pinch of salt
½ teaspoon vanilla essence (optional)

To serve

1 ripe fresh mango or seasonal fruit of your choice, peeled and cut into 1.5 cm (⅝ in) cubes
drizzle of condensed milk to garnish (optional)
toasted coconut flakes to garnish (optional)

In a pot, bring the water to a boil, add the sago and simmer for approx. 15 minutes, or until all the pearls have turned translucent. Don't worry if a few of them still have a white centre. Pour the pearls into a sieve and rinse under cold running water for about 30 seconds to stop them from sticking together. Set aside.

In a small pot, bring the coconut cream to a simmer. Turn off the heat. Stir in the maple syrup (or sugar), salt and vanilla, if using. Add the sago to the mix and stir through. Chill for at least 2 hours or overnight.

Spoon the cooled sago into serving glasses or small bowls and top with cubed fruit, a drizzle of condensed milk and a sprinkle of coconut flakes, if desired.

THE LOWDOWN

Boil sago until cooked, rinse and cool. Heat coconut cream and seasonings. Mix sago and coconut together and cool. Serve with mango. Approx. 30 minutes plus 2 hours' cooling time.

FLUFFY SOUFFLÉ PANCAKES

These soft and fluffy cake-like pancakes with their beautiful eggy aroma are great with a variety of accompaniments, from fruit to ice cream. It's a pretty simple recipe but note the little tips and tricks so they turn out great every time.

In a bowl, whisk together the egg yolks, sugar, milk, flour, vanilla and baking powder and set aside.

In a separate bowl, whisk the egg whites with an electric whisk until peaks form. It's important not to over- or under-mix the egg whites: you want stiff peaks that slowly curl down after a few seconds.

Carefully fold a little of the whites (approx 20 per cent) into the batter. When that is incorporated, slowly add more whites, 20 per cent at a time, until it's all mixed through.

Place the pancake mixture into a piping bag or sealable bag and cut the corner. Or just scoop the batter into the pan with a spoon.

Preheat a non-stick pan over a very low heat with a bit of oil, spreading it with a paper towel (or use oil spray).

If piping, first pipe 3 x 8–10 cm (3¼–4 in) rounds of the batter onto the pan and fry for 1 minute.

If spooning, spoon about 3 tablespoons of the batter for each pancake. Add 1 tablespoon of water to the side of the pan (not on the cakes) and cover with a lid to steam for 2 minutes. Pipe or spoon the same amount of batter onto the pancakes to create a thicker pancake. Add 1 tablespoon of water to the side of the pan again, cover and steam for 2–3 minutes.

When semi-firm on top, flip the pancakes over and steam for another 2–3 minutes. You know they're done when the pancakes are slightly bouncy when gently pressed.

To serve, place 2–3 pancakes per person on a plate and serve with your favourite accompaniments. Here are some of my favourite combos:

- Fresh fruit and whipped cream
- Condensed milk and butter
- Nut butters or butter and pure maple syrup

SERVES 2–3 (ABOUT 6 THICK CAKES)

4 eggs, separated
2 tablespoons caster sugar
2 tablespoons milk
½ cup high-grade flour (or baker's flour), sifted
1 teaspoon vanilla extract
½ teaspoon baking powder
oil or oil spray for cooking

THE LOWDOWN

Mix all the ingredients together, except the egg whites, to make the batter. Whip the egg whites until stiff and fold into the batter. Cook on low heat in a greased pan, covered, with splashes of water to steam. Serve with desired accompaniments. Approx. 30 minutes.

MICROWAVE MILO CAKES

As you can probably tell by now, I love using the microwave. It makes so many things so much easier, like melting, reheating, defrosting — and making things like this microwave cake in about 1 minute!

Milo is such a nostalgic flavour for me — I remember drinking it in my parents' Chinese café in Fiji and I've not really stopped.

Here's a cake you can literally make in a few minutes for those times when you don't know what to make, or for a cheeky single-serve to go with your Netflix binge. Or for when you wish you had cake lying around to go with your favourite ice cream in the freezer to impress guests.

Just multiply the recipe for however many guests you have. Pour the batter into separate bowls/mugs and microwave one at a time.

In a small bowl, mix all the ingredients, except the ice cream or cream, until well combined.

Pour the batter into a medium-sized microwave-proof bowl or large mug. The bowl/mug should be only half full. Microwave, uncovered, for 60–90 seconds depending on the strength of your microwave.

When cooked, the cake should double in height. Serve with your favourite ice cream, whipped cream or pouring cream for one of the quickest cake desserts ever.

MAKES 1 BIG PORTION

2 tablespoons flour
⅛ teaspoon baking soda
pinch of salt
3 tablespoons Milo or malt drink or hot chocolate powder
1½ tablespoons brown sugar (or any sugar)
1 egg
15 g (½ oz) butter or coconut oil, melted
ice cream or whipped or pouring cream to serve

THE LOWDOWN

Mix ingredients together for batter. Microwave batter in a large mug. Serve with ice cream or cream. Approx. 5 minutes.

MILK TEA BURNT CHEESECAKE

The idea of imperfect perfection is something I can really relate to and this dessert embodies exactly that. This Basque cheesecake is baked, burnt and deliciously ugly; it's incredibly satisfying to produce as there is no perfect way to make this and to me that *is* so perfect.

Here's my incredibly simple version with a twist of adding a milky tea flavour, drawing inspiration from Asian milk tea shops (boba shops). The tea flavour adds another layer of complexity and smells incredible. The cake is creamy, soft and surprisingly easy to make.

Preheat the oven to 210°C (410°F). Line an 18 cm (7 in) round cake tin with baking paper by taking a large piece and squishing it in and pressing on the sides (it doesn't matter if the paper overlaps in places).

Place the cream and tea leaves in a small pot over a medium heat (if using tea bags, cut the leaves into the cream). Bring to a slight simmer and then turn off. Allow the tea to infuse with the hot cream for at least 10-15 minutes, then strain the cream through a strainer into a small bowl and discard the used leaves.

In a large mixing bowl, work the sugar and cream cheese together by using a spatula to press it against the surface of the bowl. Whip and mix the two components together until softened and loosened. At this stage use a small whisk to continue whisking the mixture until it gets lighter in texture (about 3 minutes).

Add in the eggs, one at a time, whisking and mixing the batter together until everything is well incorporated. Add in the infused cream, flour and vanilla, if using. Mix well.

Pour the cake batter into the tin and bake for 26-30 minutes. The top of the cheesecake should look dark brown or blackened (no stress if it doesn't) while the cake will still be incredibly wobbly in the centre, and that is how it should be. If you feel like the cheesecake is not burnt enough, crank up the oven or grill to blacken the top for a few minutes.

Allow the cake to cool at room temperature and store in the fridge. It's best eaten after a few hours. The inside should be gooey and thick. I like to serve this with a dollop of fresh whipped cream.

SERVES 8

350 ml (12 fl oz) fresh cream
20 g (¾ oz) black tea leaves (English Breakfast, Assam or Ceylon) — or about 10 small tea bags
100 g (3½ oz) caster sugar
500 g (1 lb 2 oz) cream cheese, softened to room temperature
3 eggs
2 tablespoons flour
1 teaspoon vanilla essence — or liquid, paste or the fresh seeds from 1 vanilla pod (optional)
fresh whipped cream to serve

THE LOWDOWN

Simmer the cream with the tea leaves. Mix the sugar and cream cheese together. Whisk in the eggs, infused cream, flour and vanilla, if using. Bake in a lined cake tin. Cool overnight. Approx. 1 hour plus cooling time.

STRAWBERRIES AND CREAM SANDWICHES

Fruit-and-cream-filled sandwiches are a popular Asian snack.

This incredibly easy, not-too-sweet treat works for any occasion and for all age groups (just remove the alcohol for kids).

They are visually pleasing and make you feel less guilty than eating cake. The best part is they can be made the night before, stored in the fridge and sliced right before you serve.

Prepare the strawberries first — wash and dry and remove the stems and stalk. Slice the strawberries in half if large. Place in a bowl, add rum if using, and gently mix.

In a mixing bowl, whip the cream with a balloon or electric whisk until it is almost thick (like thick pouring gravy). Add the icing sugar, vanilla and rum, if using, and continue whisking until thick.

Spread a generous amount of cream on five slices of bread and arrange the strawberries on top, being aware of where you're going to slice the sandwiches. Fill any gaps with more cream. Spread the top slices of the bread with more cream and cover.

Individually cling-film the sandos and mark where you want to slice them. Press them down gently with a flat pan/tray and refrigerate for a minimum of 2 hours.

Unwrap and slice with a clean, sharp knife (a bread knife works well), wiping with a wet tea towel in between slices for a clean cut.

MAKES 5 SANDWICHES

500 g (1 lb 2 oz) strawberries or any ripe fresh seasonal fruit of your choice

60 ml (2 fl oz) rum for strawberries (optional)

400 ml (14 fl oz) fresh cream, super cold

¼ cup icing sugar

1 teaspoon vanilla essence

60 ml (2 fl oz) rum for cream (optional)

10 slices thick white sandwich bread or Asian milk bread or sliced brioche loaf

THE LOWDOWN

Marinate strawberries (optional). Whip seasoned cream. Place cream on sliced bread with strawberries, top with more cream and bread. Wrap and chill for 2 hours overnight. Slice. Approx. 20 minutes plus overnight cooling.

GOJI AND DATE HEALING TEA

Growing up in a Chinese household, the concept of dessert was foreign and never a part of my upbringing. Chinese banquets would either end the meal with fresh fruit or a clear sweetened broth made with rehydrated ingredients believed to contain 'healing properties' to cool down the body and restore its balance. Whether you believe in the healing aspect or not, drinking these teas always made me feel good, especially after eating way more than I should have! Also it's just a nice and refreshing tea, lightly sweetened and floral.

Soak all the dried ingredients overnight in warm water (or for 3 hours minimum) then strain, keeping the rehydrated ingredients. If your white fungus is large, rip it into smaller pieces.

Add 2 litres (70 fl oz) of water to a pot, add the jasmine tea and bring to a simmer, then remove the tea bags or leaves.

To the pot of aromatic water, add all the rehydrated ingredients and the sugar. Simmer until the sugar has dissolved, then turn off the heat.

Enjoy when cooled down. It's best chilled and served with a bit of all the rehydrated ingredients in the serving bowl or glass.

SERVES APPROX. 10

30 g (1 oz) dried goji berries

12 jujube dates (or any dried dates), pitted

20 g (¾ oz) dried white fungus (snow fungus)

30 g (1 oz) dried lotus seeds (optional)

2 litres (70 fl oz) water

4 jasmine tea bags or 8 g (¼ oz) jasmine tea leaves

80 g (2¾ oz) yellow rock sugar (or raw sugar)

THE LOWDOWN

Soak the dried ingredients overnight. In a pot with water, bring everything to a gentle simmer. Cool. Approx. 10 minutes plus overnight soaking and cooling.

MY GO-TO CITRUS COCKTAIL

When I host a dinner party for friends I usually try to make a batched cocktail for when guests arrive. Lately, I've been making this one because of how beautifully balanced it is, with the tartness of citrus, bitterness from the tonic and complexity from the gin and ginger. This is a great way to use up the leftover citrus from your fruit bowl. Remove the gin component and it makes a crazy-good complex mocktail too!

This recipe serves 1 so just multiply the ingredients for how many you want to serve. If you're making it for a dinner party, the batch can be stored in the fridge for 2–3 days in an airtight container/jar.

Make the simple sugar syrup by microwaving sugar and water in a 2:1 ratio until the sugar dissolves. For example, mix 100 g (3½ oz) sugar and 50 ml (1½ fl oz) water and microwave for 30 seconds or until the sugar is dissolved. Allow to cool.

In a jug, mix the lemon juice, orange juice, sugar syrup and grated ginger together, stirring for a 1 minute to allow the ginger to infuse into the mix. This step is optional but I like to pour the mix through a sieve at this stage to get rid of the bits of ginger so it's a sediment-free liquid for presentation.

In a glass half filled with ice, pour in the citrus mix, gin (if using) and top up with tonic. Garnish with orange peel.

SERVES 1

20 ml (½ fl oz) simple sugar syrup
30 ml (1 fl oz) freshly squeezed lemon juice
20 ml (½ fl oz) freshly squeezed orange juice
½ teaspoon grated ginger
30–60 ml (1–2 fl oz) tonic water to top up glass
30 ml (1 fl oz) gin (optional)
ice
orange peel for garnish (optional)

THE LOWDOWN

Mix all the ingredients together. Serve over ice and garnish. Approx. 10 minutes.

IMPRESSIVE MANDARIN SOUR

Here's a cocktail I enjoy making that's sure to impress any mixologist. It's sweet, aromatic and balanced, the mouthfeel from the egg white gives the drink a beautiful viscosity.

Mandarin is one of my favourite citruses because of how sweet and aromatic it is. A big part of my affinity to mandarins could be that I grew up with an infinite pile in my parents' fruit bowl, because in Chinese culture the more citrus you have in the house, the more luck it would bring.

To this day I am still obsessed with its flavour, I just use it slightly differently to how my parents would have.

Make the sugar syrup by microwaving sugar and water in a 2:1 ratio until the sugar dissolves. For example, mix 100 g (3½ oz) sugar and 50 ml (1½ fl oz) water and microwave for 30 seconds or until the sugar is dissolved. Allow to cool.

To a cocktail shaker add the juices, sugar syrup, egg white and rum or gin. Fill the shaker to about three-quarters full with ice. Seal and shake until the shaker is well frosted (about 1 minute). Double-strain the cocktail into a coupe or martini glass, shaking out as much of the foam as possible. Garnish and serve.

SERVES 1

20 ml (½ fl oz) simple sugar syrup
30 ml (1 fl oz) freshly squeezed mandarin juice
30 ml (1 fl oz) freshly squeezed lemon juice
1 egg white (or, for a vegan substitute, use 20 ml (½ fl oz) chickpea water aka aquafaba)
30 ml (1 fl oz) light rum or gin
ice
lemon balm leaf or dehydrated citrus slice to garnish (optional)

THE LOWDOWN

Make simple syrup. Shake the ingredients in a cocktail shaker with ice. Strain into cocktail glass. Approx. 10 minutes.

MY WINNING ESPRESSO MARTINI

It wouldn't feel right if I didn't feature a coffee recipe in this book since I've spent most of my professional career in that field. So here I present to you my award-winning espresso martini recipe, which won the New Zealand Coffee in Good Spirits competition hosted by the New Zealand Specialty Coffee Association in 2021.

A few simple quality ingredients make a deeply complex drink. Try to use freshly roasted beans (within a month from roast date) — it'll make a huge difference in flavour.

It's the ideal cocktail to keep you up and energetic, but mature enough for it to be classy and refined. And I think it's the perfect sign-off for the recipes in this book. Enjoy!

Make the simple sugar syrup by microwaving sugar and water in a 2:1 ratio until the sugar dissolves. For example, mix 100 g (3½ oz) dark sugar and 50 ml (1½ fl oz) water and microwave for 30 seconds or until the sugar is dissolved. Allow to cool.

Freshly extract your double-shot espresso.

In a cocktail shaker add all the ingredients, except for the garnish, and top up with ice to about three-quarters full. Seal and shake until well frosted (about 1 minute). Double strain into your favourite glass — I like using a coupe or martini glass for this. Garnish with three coffee beans or freshly grate some chocolate over the top.

SERVES 1

20 ml (½ fl oz) dark sugar syrup (use dark brown, coconut or muscovado sugar)
30 ml (1 fl oz) freshly extracted espresso (ideally with thick crema)
30 ml (1 fl oz) dark rum
20 ml (½ fl oz) coconut water
10 ml amaro or your favourite Italian spiced liqueur — I like using Amaro Montenegro
chocolate shavings or
3 coffee beans to garnish

THE LOWDOWN

Make dark sugar syrup. Extract fresh espresso. Shake all the ingredients in a cocktail shaker. Strain into cocktail glass. Garnish. Approx. 10 minutes.

THANK YOU

Writing this 'acknowledgements' section of the book is very weird and surreal for me. For the longest time I've wanted to write a cookbook — it's been a literal dream of mine, so I can't believe it's become a reality. What I did not know was how this process would change the way I think and how I choose to navigate my life as I move forward in this world, reframing and unlearning the old to make room for the new and exciting. As much as this book is about the food, people and places that have influenced me as an individual, it is in a way inherently political. Food is political.

The long emotional journey to get to where I am today has been a wild ride for sure, and it was the many people who have impacted my life who gave me the strength, confidence and self-belief to continue the work I do today.

To my mum Fong Siu Fong Low and Dad Hon Chong Low, thank you for sacrificing everything you had in China and Fiji for me and my brothers so we could have greater opportunities in life. You left behind traditions, family, friends and culture to move into a foreign world in search of a better life. Though I couldn't speak fluently to you both in a shared language with intellect and heart, we did that through food, around the table, in the kitchen, wrapping wontons by the TV and on phone calls when I was living overseas asking about nostalgic recipes. I am forever grateful for all the food memories and recipes passed onto me.

To my brothers, Norman Lum and Allan Low — I'm grateful that through all the good times and adversity, you have shaped the way I am today, making me more understanding, resilient and caring.

To my chosen family, who are pictured in the book — thank you for believing in me and reminding me that I am worthy. You all humble me and remind me that the simple things are worth living for. Melissa Liao, Tian Yang Li, Rex Chia — thank you for being there for me since the beginning. Remember that video call where I 'came out' to you all first? That was a time, eh! I was so nervous, OMG . . . now, thinking back, what a funny time that was. Love y'all!

To my close friends, new and old, thank you! You all inspire me so much. That clichéd quote, 'you are the average of your close friends', is so true! And mine just happen to be mostly queer and an incredibly talented group of POC creatives who push me to be better everyday and exist with purpose.

Ruby Jet White, thank you for your constant honesty and shared talent, not just with your gorgeous handmade ceramics (many used in the book) but also how you apply your love for food and your cultural heritage to your art.

Jean Teng — the brilliance you possess at such a young age is intoxicating. Young at heart with an old soul, I thank you for all the mentoring (especially in writing) and being my very qualified fellow food-buddy. Many more eating adventures to come for us, I hope.

Nathan Joe, thank you for being a part of this project. Your poem literally brought me to tears the first time I read it. Thank you for existing and for doing the work you do. The way you are able to create ownership and identity in everything you put your mind to with brilliance and talent is inspirational. So much love for you.

Steven Junil Park, thank you for the beautiful custom garments made for me for this project! I especially love your sense of purpose and outrageous talent — it is something I'm constantly in awe of. Thank you for teaching me to become more of my own self. (Follow Steven on IG @6x4online to see his stunning work!)

Jenna Wee, I thank you for all the life mentorship you have given and still give me, allowing me to tap into my spirituality, and for being such an anchor of support. Your work, especially with the podcast *Asian in Aotearoa* (available on most streaming platforms), gives me so much hope and inspiration for a thriving, diverse community here in New Zealand.

Amanda Grace Leo, your sense of identity and confidence is truly inspiring. Thank you for helping me foster my spirituality and believing in my own manifestations. Look at how far that's taken me!

Chris Tse, thank you for all the work you do and also the incredibly touching poem in this book. Not only are you literally the New Zealand Poet Laureate but also someone I strive to be more like. 'I wanna be more like Chris Tse when I grow up' is a constant quote in my head!

This book took an army of people and talents to put together, all adding their own influence to this collective project, from mentors to photographers.

Nadia Lim, thank you for the mentoring and believing in me since *MasterChef* to writing this book! You're such an inspiration to me.

Mel Jenkins (photographer) and Jo Bridgford (food stylist), thank you for all the beautiful food shots! With you both it felt I was able to bring my food photography desires to life. A truly professional team to work with and incredibly fun to be around! It felt like it was all play in the studio.

Vanessa Wu — thank you for taking all the stunning incidental and studio photos of me. I had so much fun working with you! I had such a strong sense of trust around you and was able to be free.

Aan Chu — thank you for all the beautiful illustrations in the book! Go follow Aan on her IG (@goodbadenglish) to see more of her stunning work. Rosabel Tan — thank you for the cultural mentorship and all the incredibly important work you do especially for the Asian community here in Aotearoa.

A huge thank you to the team from *MasterChef New Zealand* 2022, for this incredible opportunity to publish my first-ever cookbook and allowing my story to be heard. Thank you to my agents at Johnson and Laird for your constant guidance and mentorship, fighting for my worth with any project I take on.

Lastly, a huge thank you to the team at Allen & Unwin for publishing my work, especially to Jenny Hellen and Leonie Freeman for helping throughout this huge undertaking from day one, letting my vision shine and bringing something to life that hopefully will inspire many to cook my version of Chinese food at home. Thank you for the trust and believing in me, especially at moments when I had doubts.

And on a final note, I hope to have made my younger self proud. Little Sam would not have believed it was even possible for me to become someone with a voice. Yet here he is now, out and proud. It's a good reminder for us all to be kind to ourselves and look back at how far we have all come.

Much love, Sam

Index

A
Aromatic Chilli Oil 194
Asian-style Roll Cake 206

B
Banquet-style Chicken and Sweetcorn Soup 79
bao, Pork Belly Gua 49
Basic Dumpling Wrappers 58
Basic Pork Broth 70
Basic Red Chilli Oil 192
Basic Steamed Eggs 112
Beancurd-fermented Chinese Cabbage 40
beef
  Braised Beef Brisket with Daikon 184
  Spicy Black Bean Beef 183
  Spicy Saucy Tofu 104
Blanched Gai Lan with Oyster Sauce 91
Blue Cod with Sizzling Oil, Steamed 159
Bok Choy Stir-fry 88
Braised Beek Brisket with Daikon 184
brownie, Gooey Chocolate and Mochi Brownie 210

C
cabbage
  Beancurd-fermented Chinese Cabbage 40
  Quick Stir-fried Cabbage 87
  Sichuan-style Pickles 39
  Tomato and Fermented Cabbage Omelette Rice 132
cake
  Asian-style Roll Cake 206
  Chinese Brown Sugar Steamed Cake 209
  Microwave Milo Cakes 219
  Milk Tea Burnt Cheesecake 220
Cantonese Congee 125
Cantonese-inspired Quick Pickles 37
cheesecake, Milk Tea Burnt 220
chicken
  Banquet-style Chicken and Sweetcorn Soup 79
  Chicken and Sweetcorn Dumpling Filling 56
  Chicken Broth (variation on Basic Pork Broth) 72
  Chicken Congee 127
  Chicken Mince (Basic Steamed Eggs Topping) 114
  Classic Chinese Poached Chicken 188
  Spicy Kung Pao Chicken 187
  Supreme Chicken Master Broth 75

chilli
  Aromatic Chilli Oil 194
  Basic Red Chilli Oil 192
  Chilli Soy Sauce 188
  Easy Hot and Sour Soup 82
  Sichuan-style Pickles 39
  Simple Cumin and Chilli Lamb Skewers 179
  Simple Spicy and Tangy Stir-fry Potato 95
  Spicy Black Bean Beef 183
  Spicy Kung Pao Chicken 187
  Spicy Saucy Tofu 104
  Steamed Salmon in Chilli Bean Sauce 153
  Ultimate Chilli Crisp Oil, The 195
  Ultimate Spicy and Tangy Stir-fry Potato 96
  XL Cumin and Chilli Lamb Skewers 180
Chinese Brown Sugar Steamed Cake 209
Chinese Chive Omelette 117
Chocolate and Mochi Brownie, Gooey 210
Classic Chinese Poached Chicken 188
Classic Dumpling 52
cocktail
  Impressive Mandarin Sour 228

My Go-to Citrus Cocktail 227
My Winning Espresso Martini 231
Coconut Sago, Easy 213
congee
  Cantonese Congee 125
  Chicken Congee 127
  Fish Congee 127
  Pork and Century Egg Congee 128
Creamy Peanut Butter Noodles 136
Crispy Cantonese-style Pork Belly 168
Cucumber Salad, Smashed 43

D
Dan Dan Noodles, Saucy 140
Date Healing Tea, Goji and 225
dumpling
  Basic Dumpling Wrappers 58
  Chicken and Sweetcorn Dumpling Filling 56
  Classic Dumpling 52
  Dumplings Pan-fried with a Crispy Base 65
  Pork and Prawn Dumpling Filling 54
  Tofu and Mushroom Dumpling Filling 57

E
Easy Coconut Sago 213
Easy Hot and Sour Soup 82
Easy Steamed Fish Fillets 156
egg
  Basic Steamed Eggs 112
  Chinese Chive Omelette 117
  Oyster Omelette 118
  Pork and Century Egg Congee 128
  Tea-soaked Soy Eggs 111
  Tomato and Fermented Cabbage Omelette Rice 132
  Tomato Egg 108
eggplant, Fragrant Saucy 100
Espresso Martini, My Winning 231
Exploding Ginger and Spring Onion Relish 196

F
Fish Congee 127
Fish Fillets, Easy Steamed 156
Fluffy Soufflé Pancakes 216
Fragrant Saucy Eggplant 100
Fungus Salad, Wood Ear 45

G
Gai Lan with Oyster Sauce, Blanched 91
Goji and Date Healing Tea 225
Gooey Chocolate and Mochi Brownie 210
gravy
  Soy Gravy 103
  Soy Shiitake Gravy 115

H
Honey Walnut Shrimp 164
Hot and Sour Soup, Easy 82

I
Impressive Mandarin Sour 228

J
Juicy Prawn Toast 46

K
Kung Pao Chicken, Spicy 187
lamb
  Lamb Skewers, Simple Cumin and Chilli 179
  XL Cumin and Chilli Lamb Skewers 180

M
Mandarin Sour, Impressive 228
Martini, My Winning Espresso 231
Master Broth, Supreme Chicken 75
Microwave Milo Cakes 219
Milk Tea Burnt Cheesecake 220
Milo Cakes, Microwave 219
mushroom
  Easy Hot and Sour Soup 82
  Goji and Date Healing Tea 225
  Soy Shiitake Gravy (Basic Steamed Eggs Topping) 115
  Tofu and Mushroom Dumpling Filling 57
  Wood Ear Fungus Salad 45
My Go-to Citrus Cocktail 227
My Winning Espresso Martini 231

O
oil
  Aromatic Chilli Oil 194
  Ultimate Chilli Crisp Oil, The 195

omelette
  Chinese Chive Omelette 117
  oyster Omelette 118
  Tomato and Fermented Cabbage Omelette Rice 132
oysters
  Oyster Omelette 118
  Steamed Oysters with Vermicelli and Exploded Aromatics 150

P
pancakes, Fluffy Soufflé 216
Peanut Butter Noodles, Creamy 136
pickles
  Cantonese-inspired Quick Pickles 37
  Sichuan-style Pickles 39
Plain Rice 122
poached chicken, Classic Chinese 188
pork
  Basic Pork Broth 70
  Crispy Cantonese-style Pork Belly 168
  Pork and Century Egg Congee 128
  Pork and Prawn Dumpling Filling 54
  Pork Belly Gua Bao 49
  Pork Mince (Basic Steamed Eggs Topping) 114
  Pork Strips (variation on Easy Hot and Sour Soup) 83
  Pork-Stuffed Peppers with Soy Gravy 103
  Red-Braised Pork Belly 172
  Saucy Dan Dan Noodles 140
  Twice-cooked Pork with Cumin 175
potato
  Simple Spicy and Tangy Stir-fry Potato 95
  Ultimate Spicy and Tangy Stir-fry Potato, The 96
prawn
  Pork and Prawn Dumpling Filling 54
  Prawn Toast, Juicy 46

Q
Quick and Easy Spring Onion Oil Noodles 139
Quick and Easy Sweetcorn Soup 76
Quick Stir-fried Cabbage 87

R
Red-braised Pork Belly 172
relish, Exploding Ginger and Spring Onion 196

S
Sago, Easy Coconut 213
salad
  Smashed Cucumber Salad 43
  Vibrant Seafood Prosperity salad 146
  Wood Ear Fungus Salad 45
Salmon in Chilli Bean Sauce, Steamed 153
Salt and Pepper Fried Tofu 107
Salt and Pepper Squid 163
sandwiches, Strawberries and Cream 222
sauce
  Chilli Sauce 153
  Chilli Soy Sauce 188
  Plum Sauce 146
  Seasoning Sauce 149
  Strange Flavour Sauce 201
  Sweet Fragrant Soy Sauce 202
Saucy Dan Dan Noodles 140
Scallops in Gravy (Basic Steamed Egg Topping) 114
Shrimp, Honey Walnut 164
Sichuan-style Pickles 39
Simple Cumin and Chilli Lamb Skewers 179
Simple Dry-fry Green Beans 99
Simple Spicy and Tangy Stir-fry Potato 95
Smashed Cucumber Salad 43
Sour, Impressive Mandarin 228
Soy Gravy 103
Soy Shiitake Gravy (Basic Steamed Eggs Topping) 115
Spam Fried Rice 135
Spicy Black Bean Beef 183
Spicy Kung Pao Chicken 187
Spicy Saucy Tofu 104
squid
  Salt and Pepper Squid 163
  Squid with Celery 160
Steamed Blue Cod with Sizzling Oil 159
Steamed Oysters with Vermicelli and Exploded Aromatics 150
Steamed Salmon in Chilli Bean Sauce 153
Strange Flavour Sauce 201
Strawberries and Cream Sandwiches 222
Supreme Chicken Master Broth 75

Sweet Fragrant Soy Sauce 202
sweetcorn
  Banquet-style Chicken and Sweetcorn Soup 79
  Chicken and Sweetcorn Dumpling Filling 56
  Quick and Easy Sweetcorn Soup 76

T
tea
  Goji and Date Healing Tea 225
  Milk Tea Burnt Cheesecake 220
  Tea-soaked Soy Eggs 111
tofu
  Salt and Pepper Fried Tofu 107
  Spicy Saucy Tofu 104
  Tofu and Mushroom Dumpling Filling 57
tomato
  Easy Hot and Sour Soup 82
  Tomato and Fermented Cabbage Omelette Rice 132
  Tomato Egg 108
  Tomato Rice 132
Twice-cooked Pork with Cumin 175

U
Ultimate Chilli Crisp Oil, The 195
Ultimate Spicy and Tangy Stir-fry Potato, The 96

V
Vibrant Seafood Prosperity Salad 146

W
Watercress Cooked in Broth 92
Wontons, Fried 146
Wood Ear Fungus Salad 45

X
XL Cumin and Chilli Lamb Skewers 180

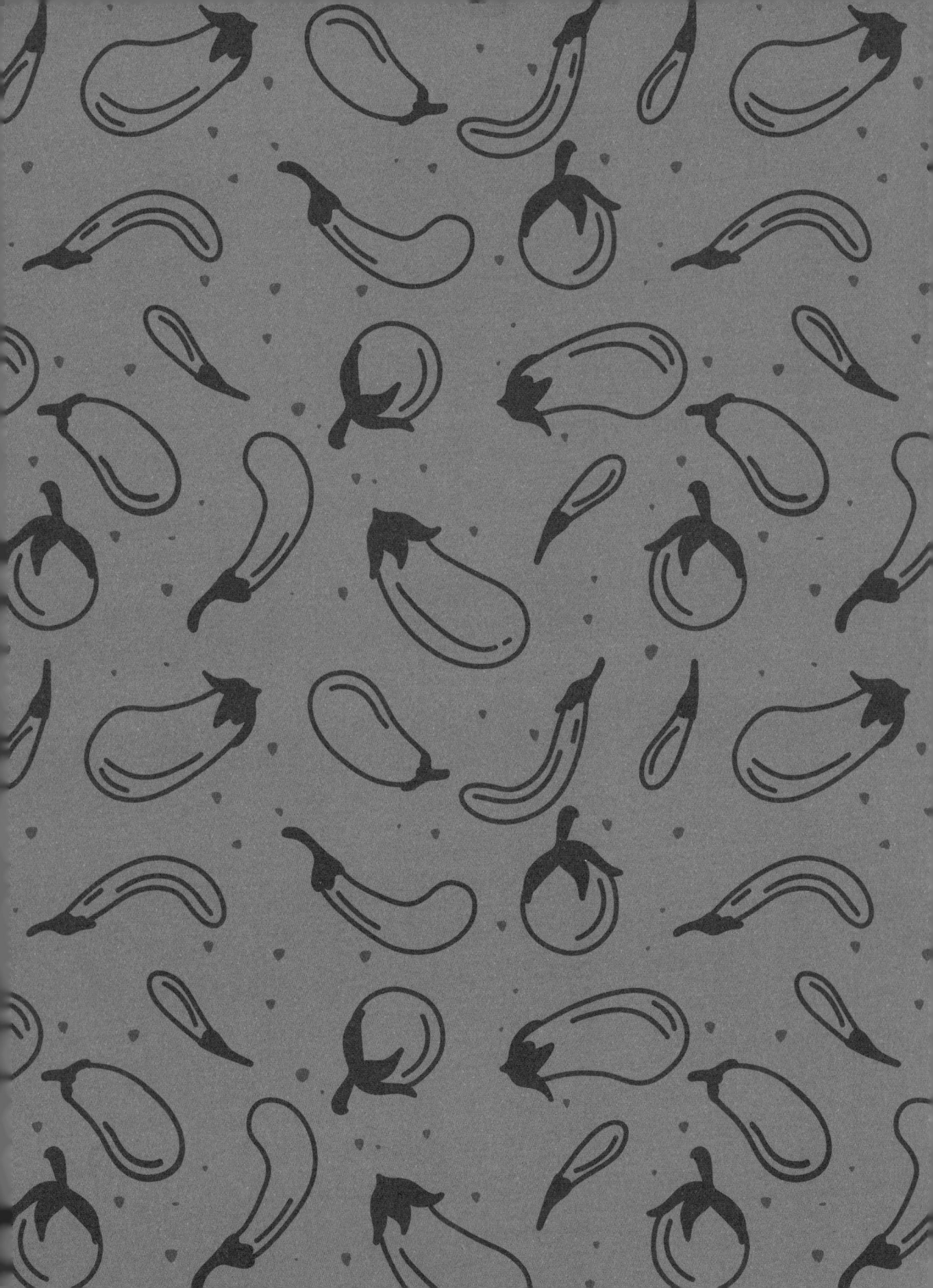